Contents

P9-DHL-370

The Self–Control Classroom

Understanding and Managing
the Disruptive Behavior of all Students,
Including Those with ADHD

James Levin
John M. Shanken–Kaye

KENDALL/HUNT PUBLISHING COMPANY
4050 Westmark Drive   Dubuque, Iowa 52002

Copyright © 1996 by James Levin and John Shanken-Kaye

ISBN 0-7872-4853-3

All rights reserved. No part of this publication may be reproduced,
stored in a retrieval system, or transmitted, in any form or by any
means, electronic, mechanical, photocopying, recording, or otherwise,
without the prior written permission of the copyright owner.

Printed in the United States of America
10 9 8 7 6 5

Dedication

This book is dedicated to the women we love:

Andy,

Carolyn,

Heidi,

Sarah,

and

Sommer

Acknowledgments

The authors gratefully acknowledge the patience, understanding, and support of their wives, Carolyn and Andy, and their children, Sommer, Heidi and Sarah. The book was written over many weekends away from home (see below), seriously taxing all concerned. We could not have accomplished the task without the unwavering and enthusiastic backing of our families. We promise never to leave home again.

Dr. Andrea Commaker, our editor and the founder of *The Society for the Proper Use of Colons and Semi-Colons*, performed a miraculous feat, in convincing two very headstrong writers that their writing could stand some improvement. We are convalescing nicely, and should be recovered in time for our next volume: *Control Yourself and Don't Argue with your Editor*.

Dr. William Beisel, the director of the Williamsport, PA center for Penn State Continuing Education, was instrumental in providing a forum to the authors in which to develop and refine our concepts. (Next time lunch is on us, Bill.)

Lastly, we would like to thank the staff and management of The Hotel Hershey, Hershey, PA, for providing a most excellent home away from home during the writing of this book.

Notes About the Structure of the Book

This book has three major divisions. The first contains the philosophies and concepts that form the foundation of our approach to the management of children with difficult behavioral problems. This division encompasses Chapters 1 through 5.

The second division, Chapter 6, is the prevention of management problems through the design and use of effective instructional and motivational strategies. Included is the development of educational climates which enhance a students' intrinsic motivation.

The management of disruptive student behavior, covered in Chapters 7-9, is the third division. The methodologies developed and chosen for this section are those which respect student self-control. The approach to disruptive behavior is developed as a hierarchy of interventions moving from less to more teacher/student confrontation as the disruptive behavior moves from common, in Chapter 7, to chronic, in Chapter 9.

Activities designed to encourage readers to develop their understanding of the philosophies and concepts discussed are used throughout the book. These activities are similar to those we, the authors, use in our workshops. Participants at these workshops indicate that the activities are very helpful, and we therefore encourage you to take the time to complete them.

Studying the many tables, charts, and figures will help readers gain a deeper understanding of the relationships among the various concepts explored in this book.

Each chapter ends with a concept map and frequently asked questions. The concept maps diagram the authors' understanding of how the major concepts in each chapter are interrelated. Your understanding is apt to be different from the authors', and so we encourage you to try your hand at developing your own concept maps. This exercise will yield a deeper understanding of the concepts developed in each chapter.

The frequently asked questions were culled from submissions of participants at our workshops. Taking the time to provide your own answers will require incorporating the knowledge gained from reading this book into your own existing understanding of best professional teaching practice.

Preface

Unlike most books on classroom management and/or Attention Deficit Hyperactivity Disorder (ADHD), we do not merely provide long lists of techniques, hints, and/or tips of the day, for the management of students. While we recognize that these tips may be helpful, we believe that what teachers most need is not only additional techniques or gimmicks, but knowledge of the underlying processes that foster student learning and behavioral management.

If You Know the *Whys*, You Can Develop the *Hows*

Teachers are professionals whose expertise is derived from a detailed and rich knowledge base. Teachers are decision makers. One of the primary difficulties with texts that are written in the *How To . . .* format as in, *How To Manage The Behavior of Disruptive Children*, is that they treat the classroom teacher as a technician, not as a professional.

Technicians only follow procedures and routines designed by others; professionals develop and implement procedures and routines from their knowledge base, as well as using their knowledge base to critically evaluate and choose techniques developed by others. Technicians, once they have applied all the procedures and routines, are frequently at a loss to determine what to do next if they have not accomplished their goals. Professionals continuously are able to draw upon their knowledge base to adapt and change procedures and routines to best meet the demands of new and unique situations.

When classroom management is viewed as a series of techniques, as it often is by writers of texts about difficult students, the classroom teacher is viewed merely as a technician. Once the teacher subscribes to this view, she is frequently at a loss to determine what to do when she runs out of techniques.

According to the philosopher Nietzsche, If a man knows the *why*, he can bear any *how*. We believe that if you know the *whys*, you can develop the *hows*.

Therefore, what this book advocates and provides is first, insuring that you, the regular classroom teacher, know the *whys*, in other words, have an enriched knowledge base. Secondly, that you develop the confidence effectively to reference and to use this knowledge to design and carry out the *hows*, the appropriate instructional and management strategies. The following nine chapters are about the effective management and instruction of all children, with an emphasis upon children with behavioral difficulties including those with ADHD. Experts estimate that 80 percent of all children with these difficulties effectively can be instructed and managed in the inclusive classroom (Kauffman, et al., 1995). Our concerns here are the instruction and management of the children who comprise only this 80 percent and not the remaining 20 percent of children who are so seriously emotionally or behaviorally disordered that they need specialized educational placements, settings, and programs.

We, the authors, anticipate and hope that after you read this book and understand and apply its concepts, you will be more effective and feel more comfortable with your professional role in managing all children, even those with difficult behavioral problems. If you have any comments we would welcome your input.

Kauffman, J. M., Lloyd, J. W., Baker, J., and Reidel, T. M., (1995). Inclusion of all students with emotional or behavioral disorders? Let's think again. *Phi Delta Kappan*, 76, 7, 542-546.

Chapter I

Basic Philosophies and Definitions

INTRODUCTION

Perhaps this conversation which takes place in a faculty lounge sounds familiar to you. One teacher is heard saying to another teacher, "This year has been great. I really feel that I was successful in reaching my students. But I can't tell you how much I'm dreading September. I just learned that in my new class I have one boy with ADHD and a girl whose temper tantrums are legendary. They're going to mess up all my teaching plans. I'm not trained to deal with these kids. What am I going to do?"

This quotation, in which the teacher feels that she lacks the necessary specific training to teach students with behavioral problems and/or ADHD, illustrates a commonly held misconception of many teachers. The misconception is that a specialized body of knowledge exists for dealing effectively with these students, dictating vastly different instructional and management techniques from those that are effective with the so-called regular student. Feelings of general ineffectiveness due to the supposed lack of knowledge causes teachers who work with these children to report higher levels of stress and frustration than other teachers. These feelings are so strong and ingrained in many teachers' thinking that for some, like the teacher in our example, just the anticipation of having one of these students placed in their classroom is enough to cause anxiety and fear.

Certainly students with behavioral difficulties do pose serious academic and behavioral problems for teachers. However we believe that to manage these problems, a teacher does not have to have any specialized instructional or management knowledge base vastly different than what is effective for other students. Most teachers already have some degree of the necessary knowledge and skills, but they must increase their knowledge and skills and must also become more effective in using all of them. However both their preconceived notions, such as those held by the teacher in the faculty lounge, and their increased stress and anxiety, which that teacher also felt, are formidable barriers to their effectiveness.

The first step in eliminating these barriers is for you to restructure the way you think about disruptive students, and indeed about the management of all students and the role you play in their education. Formally such a process is called *cognitive restructuring,* that is, challenging or reframing the way you think. If this book is successful in helping you to restructure your cognitions, then you will be ready to make significant changes in how you instruct and manage students with behavioral problems. You will feel more effective and less stressed and anxious. Your classroom will become a more successful learning environment, not only for difficult students, but for all students.

Therefore lies our primary underlying philosophy: There is nothing vastly different in instruction and management that you need to do with disruptive students, including those with ADHD. You just have to do it better!

This chapter starts the process of your cognitive restructuring. We begin to provide the *whys* of effective management in the classroom by: 1) describing the philosophical foundations of effective management, 2) explaining the process by which teachers become emotionally tied to students' behaviors, 3) defining the teaching/learning process, and 4) defining the behavioral characteristics that differentiate discipline problems from the many other behavioral problems found in the classroom.

PHILOSOPHIES

Think about the individuals in your life whom you control. For many of you this list may include your children, spouse, students, and classroom aides. How many of these people do precisely as you desire all of the time? Are they inescapably tied to your demands, and have they no other choice but to follow your instructions?

As you re-think the issue of whom you control, it becomes obvious that you have control over no one's behavior but your own. This is not to say that you are powerless in affecting people's behavior, but you do not have control. What you do have is influence. If you had control, your immediate surroundings would be perfect, because you would be surrounded by students, children, spouses, and co-workers all doing exactly as you desired all the time. All you would have to do is issue a request and those around you would comply. Now, wouldn't that make your world lovely?

The distinction between control and influence is not one merely of semantics. This misconception of how much control we think we have over other people's behavior is what causes the stress and frustration that many of us feel in our personal and professional lives.

So you say, "OK, fine. I don't have control. What I have is influence. But when I tell a kid to be quiet, that kid better be quiet. If she doesn't then I'm going to . . .." However, most teachers we come in contact with are quick to point out that just because they demand a student stop talking, does not insure compliance, and, in some cases, the student's talking may actually escalate.

What happens when the student doesn't comply? If you are honest with yourself, you realize that there is not much you can do that guarantees compliance. Granted, you can make additional demands, use time out, call parents, remove privileges, and refer to the office. While these techniques might be effective in gaining the desired result in the short term, rarely do they yield long term success.

So, do you have control? We would argue not really.

Self Control vs. Control of Students

You may now be thinking about that teacher down the hall from you who doesn't scream or give detentions, and yet the students in her classroom are consistently well behaved. Surely that teacher has control. We agree that she does have extraordinary control. However, she does not have control over her students. She has control over her own behavior. By controlling her own behavior, she influences in significant ways how her students are choosing to behave.

It is our belief that the only person you can control is yourself, and depending on how you choose to behave, you influence how the people around you, including your students, choose to behave. This powerful concept of teacher self-control is stressed throughout this book.

It is reasonable for you to ask, "Since I can only control my own behavior, how do I decide what my behavior should be? What changes should I make to influence students to choose to act appropriately?" When addressing complex issues, other experts are quick to offer advice on what not to do before suggesting what to do; so, we have decided to keep with tradition and discuss what not to do first.

What not to do is clearly illustrated by one of the author's first teaching experiences over twenty years ago. He taught secondary mathematics in a large inner city junior high school. Assigned five classes and supervised by the assistant principal, this author started his career as an educator. Four of the classes were fine, but the fifth was plagued by extensive behavioral problems. This class was never without disruptive behavior. Lateness to class, calling out, walking around the room, name calling, and hitting were common. In addition, there were some unforgettable behaviors, such as a young lady displaying her displeasure with a young man's put down by standing on her desk, pulling her pants down, and telling the young man to "kiss her ass."

The author was supervised by an assistant principal who noted everything that occurred, but who believed in waiting for the teachable moment and so did not intervene. Because the author was too proud to seek the experienced help of this supervisor, he continued to endure this class along with feelings of inadequacy, stress, and the accompanying headaches and stomachaches it engendered.

As Thanksgiving rapidly approached, the author finally requested a meeting with the assistant principal. He admitted to her that he was unable to control the students in this class and was seriously considering leaving the profession of teaching at the end of the year. The assistant principal calmly replied, "I've been waiting months for you to ask me about this problem. Rather than speaking about control, tell me what methods you've tried so far to manage these students' behavior?" Almost ready to explode, the author replied, "I fail them and they don't care. I call their parents, but rarely are they home and never do they return my calls. I change their seats but they refuse to move. I scream at them but they ignore me. I give them detentions but they don't come. Whatever it takes, I don't have it."

Unfazed but in a supportive tone, the assistant principal replied, "You cannot control someone else. You can control only yourself." She went on to say, **"If you continue to do what you're doing, you'll continue to get what you got."** Thus, this author learned what not to do. He could not continue to do what he was doing. The same applies to you. If you are dissatisfied with what you *got* (student behavior), you must change what you are doing.

You may now be getting a little irritated thinking, "It's easy to say change what I'm doing, but this still hasn't answered the question: What should I be doing?" It is a simple fact that we all do what we know how to do. In addition, our behaviors are usually congruent with our belief system; that is, we behave in ways which do not cause us to question our long held beliefs. For example, if we support welfare programs, then we probably believe that people want to work, but that some people are so disadvantaged that they can't find jobs. On the other hand, if we are opposed to welfare programs, we probably believe that those without jobs choose not to work and are just plain lazy or have moral deficits. It would be very unlikely that a person would simultaneously support welfare programs and also believe that able bodied people who did not work were just plain lazy.

Relating the impact of our beliefs to how we teach difficult students, we believe that we should be able to control the students in our classrooms, and so we use strategies to force students to change their behavior. On the other hand, we are daily shown that these teacher behaviors are ineffective. Clinging to our beliefs however, we continue to use failed strategies and/or cast about for coercive techniques that promise to increase our effectiveness. What we must do instead is challenge the underlying belief that students should and can be controlled.

What is then the answer to the question, "What should I be doing?" We suggest that the answer begins with changing your mind, because "If you can't change your mind, then you can't change anything." Changing your mind begins with obtaining accurate information which challenges your beliefs about why students misbehave, the nature of teaching, learning, and discipline problems, and how you can intervene effectively.

This book will help you change your mind, in other words, engage in cognitive restructuring. When this occurs you will be amazed at how your behavior changes, your effectiveness increases, and your stress level is reduced. Then you will be in the position to effectively manage and instruct all the students in your classroom. When you are an effective teacher for students with behavioral problems, you are an exceptional teacher for all the other students. Therefore, everyone in your classroom benefits.

To summarize, the philosophical foundations of this book begin with a basic premise: if you continue to do what you've done, then you'll continue to get what you've got. Since the great majority of the readers of this book are probably not satisfied with the results they have gotten, the authors assume that they desire a change. This change must be in your behavior, because the only behavior you can control is your own. Finally, behavioral change can be strange and uncomfortable, especially if the behavioral change is not congruent with your belief system. Thus, you must first change the way you think about student behavior and teacher behavior, because if you can't change your mind, then you can't change anything.

FOUNDATIONAL CONCEPTS

The Emotional Aspects of Management: The Parallel Process

How do you feel when you are confronted with a chronically disruptive student? Think about the 50th time you've intervened for the same type of behavior in the last 3 months. Take a moment to list some of the emotions you might feel given this scenario.

_____   _____   _____   _____

_____   _____   _____   _____

We have asked hundreds of students how they felt when being corrected by a teacher for the umpteenth time for the same behavior. Some examples of their responses include being frustrated, angry, resentful, hopeless, depressed, upset (especially in the stomach), incompetent, insignificant, powerless, vengeful, and generally aggravated.

Do you notice anything the two lists have in common? If you are like the thousands of teachers with whom we have worked, the comparison indicates marked similarities between how you and the student feel under the same circumstances.

If you are caught up in these unpleasant emotions, are you likely to use well thought out professional approaches which maximize the probability of the student regaining self-control? Probably not. How about the student who is experiencing similar feelings? Will she likely respond to the teacher's intervention in a manner that decreases the likelihood for further unpleasant interactions? Again, probably not.

This phenomenon of shared affective experience is called a *parallel process*. Many times when teachers and students interact, what the teacher experiences on an affective level is the same or similar to what the student experiences. This shared experience may either interfere with successful interventions by creating a spiral of hostility and suspicion between the teacher and the student or it may create a shared expectation of positive growth. In order for positive growth to occur, one of the parties in this process must become aware of the cycle and decide to act to interfere in a positive manner. This person is unlikely to be the student. Therefore, it needs to be you.

As an adult you have a greater understanding of causes, a greater ability to see future possibilities, and, most importantly, because you are a teaching professional, you have the responsibility to use your greater capabilities to change your behavior to increase the likelihood of a positive outcome. A participant at one of our workshops paraphrased William Glasser, an expert on classroom management, "We do not have a responsibility for students, but we have a responsibility to students." Teachers do not have a responsibility for the behavior of their students. Rather they have a responsibility to use professional behavior to increase the likelihood that students behave appropriately.

The next time that you feel an emotional response to a student's behavior, keep the parallel process in mind. There is a high probability that the student is feeling the same way. You very well may recognize the same emotions played out on her face. Then ask yourself, "What behavior on the part of this student would have to change to increase the likelihood of my mood improving?" When you have the answer, behave that way toward your student. You may find yourself pleasantly surprised at the results.

Reflecting upon your feelings to accurately identify and empathize with your student's feelings is what psychologists term *accurate empathy*. Understanding the concept of the parallel process and using accurate empathy greatly increases the efficacy of any interactions you have with your students.

Definitions of Learning, Teaching, and Discipline Problems

Learning

As a professional educator, your primary interest is in helping students learn. However, have you ever thought about the definition of learning? Near the end of a workshop that the authors were facilitating, a teacher asked, "How do you know if a student has learned?" At first we were surprised by such a question, assuming that the answer was obvious to seasoned educators. However, we decided that defining learning was a necessary beginning point for future workshops and began to ask participants to define learning. To our surprise, the answer to this question was not obvious to teachers. The question was usually met with vague definitions or silence.

To assist teachers in formulating the definition of learning, we usually use the example of how athletics or drama is taught. When teachers who coach teams or direct plays are asked how they know if their students have learned the athletic plays or the drama parts, they respond, "The students run the plays or act out their parts." In other words, the students are able to exhibit a behavior that they were unable to display before. Therefore, these teachers are saying that learning is an observable change in behavior. While it is true that learning may occur even if students do not display a change in behavior, it is impossible for teachers to know that learning has occurred unless they observe a change in the student's behavior. Obviously, the change in behavior cannot be random but must be congruent with the learning goal. It must be behavior that is expected if the student learned the content of the lesson.

Most teachers limit this definition of learning to the academic domain. However, this definition is also applicable when discussing disruptive behavior. If a student can not write an introductory paragraph in English, she must learn how to do this. The teacher will deduce that this learning has taken place when the student changes her behavior in an observable way, that is, writes a correct introductory paragraph. Similarly, if a student during cooperative group work continually walks around the room disrupting other student groups, she must learn how to sit with her group as a first step in cooperatively working with the assigned group without disrupting other students. In fact, the student may know how to sit and work cooperatively in a group, but the teacher is unable to state that this behavior has been learned until the teacher observes the student's behavioral change. Thus, learning is an observable change in any behavior, academic, affective, social, or psychomotor.

Teaching

Now that a definition of learning has been developed, consider the question, "What is teaching?" Many teachers respond to this question as they do to the question about learning, with vague descriptions or silence. Common responses include giving information, delivery of knowledge, and transferring information. These definitions are inadequate, because they do not include how knowledge is specifically transferred. These definitions also limit teaching to the cognitive domain.

When teachers limit the concept of teaching solely to the cognitive domain, they limit their effectiveness in managing disruptive students. Disruptive students, like all students, need to develop cognitively. However, they also need to develop affectively. In particular, disruptive students need to learn how to express negative affects such as anger, boredom, and frustration in a manner that is not disruptive to other students or the teacher. If they are not successful in learning self-management, their cognitive development will most likely suffer. Teachers who understand this broader notion of teaching to include components of the affective as well as the cognitive domain are in a better position to work effectively with disruptive students. To the extent that teachers accept the proposition that facilitating affective development is an important part of teaching rather than a disruption of the teaching process, they are less likely to view the needed interventions as a waste of time. These teachers are therefore less likely to become frustrated and otherwise stressed when working with students who pose difficult behavioral challenges.

The idea that teaching extends beyond the academic realm was illustrated at a recent seminar when a participant offered the following definition of teaching. She said that teaching was "being a change agent of student behavior." This definition does recognize that all student behavior is included. It does relate teaching to the definition of learning, an observable change in behavior. However, the definition is limited in that it does not include the means by which teachers facilitate students' behavioral change. How do we attempt to change student behavior? If we answer this question, we are well on our way to defining teaching.

To answer the above question we first must analyze what teachers do when students are having difficulty learning. For example, you teach a lesson on long division using direct teacher instruction. Then you give out a worksheet to students so they may practice this new skill. As you walk around the room to see how the students are doing, you notice that Gina is unable to successfully complete any long division problems. Her long division behavior has not changed; she has not learned. What will you now do? Most teachers say they will reteach the steps of long division to Gina and then reassess. Suppose after you do this, you again determine that Gina did not get it. Most teachers come up with strategies such as peer instruction or the use of manipulatives. The important point here is that when the student isn't learning, (changing her long division behavior), the teacher must change the teaching strategy. In other words, the teacher changes her behavior.

We are now close to formally defining teaching, but there is one more factor we must consider. If you want students to change their behaviors, you have to change your behavior. However, the behavior that you decide to employ is one that maximizes the likelihood that student behavior will change in the appropriate way. Concerning Gina's difficulty with long division, the teacher hopefully changes her teaching in a manner that increases the likelihood that Gina will learn long division. The probability of choosing the most effective teaching behavior increases when the teacher's behavior is not random or haphazard, but instead is based upon a professional knowledge base including how children learn, motivation theory, child development, pedagogy, and experience (Brophy, 1988).

Gina having difficulty with long division is analogous to Alisha having difficulty staying in her seat, raising her hand, or lining up quietly for a fire drill. The application of the process of teaching to these latter behaviors is also similar and begins with the same question. The teacher must ask herself, "In what ways can I change my behavior to increase the likelihood of the student changing her behavior?" Thus, just as a teacher changes her behavior to increase the likelihood of a student being able to successfully complete long division problems, a teacher must also change her behavior to increase the likelihood that the student remains seated, raises her hand to answer, or lines up properly for a fire drill.

Putting together all of the pieces, the definition of teaching is changing teacher behavior in a manner that increases the likelihood that students will change their behavior. Formally stated, "teaching is the use of preplanned behaviors, founded in learning principles and child development theory and directed toward both instructional delivery and classroom management, which increases the probability of effecting a positive change in student behavior" (Levin and Nolan, 1996, p. 4).

To summarize the major points of this definition of teaching:

1. You cannot force a student to behave; you can only influence the change;
2. To influence a change in student behavior, you must change your behavior, because this is the only behavior over which you have control;
3. The behavior you choose will have a much higher probability of influencing positive student behavior if you examine and use your professional knowledge base in making the choice;

4. This process of teaching is the same if the student is having cognitive or affective problems; and

5. The change in your behavior increases only the likelihood of the desired change in student behavior, but it does not cause the desired change.

While all five points of the definition are important, # 2 is the heart of the definition as it clearly stresses that the only mechanism you have as a teacher to influence a change in student behavior is your own behavior.

Discipline Problems

The difficulty many teachers have with defining learning and teaching is also evident when they attempt to categorize behaviors that are discipline problems. Teachers often describe students whom they believe have discipline problems as being lazy, unmotivated, angry, argumentative, and aggressive. These descriptions are imprecise and judgmental. They communicate nothing about the actual behavior that is considered to be the discipline problem. These descriptions are also problematic because we all know students who are lazy or unmotivated, yet their classroom behaviors do not constitute discipline problems. In addition, these words personalize the misbehavior by focusing on the characteristics of the individual student. This violates a general guideline offered by Ginott (1972), "Speak to the situation not to the person." Because of these attributions, teachers develop negative feelings toward the student as a person (Brendtro, et al., 1990) which greatly reduces a teacher's effectiveness in working with the student to modify the student's behavior.

An operational definition must provide a teacher with behavioral criteria in order that an instantaneous decision may be made whether or not any given behavior is a discipline problem. If it is, the teacher then needs to make a professional decision concerning which management strategies to employ to increase the likelihood that the student will change her behavior to a more appropriate one. In other words, once a behavior is identified as a discipline problem, the teacher needs to change her behavior or needs to teach.

So what is the definition of a discipline problem? Let's analyze five common classroom scenarios to develop an operational definition. To aid in this analysis, ask yourself three questions after you read each scenario, and fill in Table1.1 with your answers.

1. Is there a discipline problem?
2. If so, who is exhibiting the discipline problem?
3. What, if there is any, is the disruptive behavior?

Scenario 1: Students enter the classroom and take their seats. The teacher asks them to take out their homework. The teacher notices that Carla has not taken out her homework but is instead playing with the rubber bands and erasers that she managed to accumulate in her desk. *The teacher ignores Carla and begins to involve the class in answering the homework problems.*

Scenario 2: Students enter the classroom and take their seats. The teacher asks them to take out their homework. The teacher notices that Carla has not taken out her homework but is instead playing with the rubber bands and erasers that she managed to accumulate in her desk. *The teacher stops the review, continues to stand in the front of the class, and publicly says,*

"Carla, put the rubber bands away and get out your assignment for this class! We will not continue until you do so!"

Scenario 3: Students enter the classroom and take their seats. The teacher asks them to take out their homework. The teacher notices that Carla has not taken out her homework but is instead playing with the rubber bands and erasers that she managed to accumulate in her desk. *The teacher begins to involve the class in answering the homework problems. As the homework is being reviewed, the teacher stands next to Carla and continues to involve the class in the homework review.*

Scenario 4: Students enter the classroom and take their seats. The teacher asks them to take out their homework. Instead Carla begins to shoot little bits of paper at her neighbors with the rubber bands that she has accumulated in her desk. *The teacher ignores this behavior and continues to review the homework. Carla continues shooting the wads of paper at the other students.*

Scenario 5: Students enter the classroom and take their seats. The teacher asks them to take out their homework. Instead Carla begins to shoot little bits of paper at her neighbors with the rubber bands that she has accumulated in her desk. *The teacher while reviewing the homework makes eye contact with Carla, but Carla continues to shoot the paper. Next the teacher walks up to Carla, takes the rubber band and paper, and as privately as possible assertively asks Carla to please take out her homework, standing next to her until she does.*

TABLE 1.1 *Who Is the Discipline Problem?*

QUESTION	SCENARIO 1	SCENARIO 2	SCENARIO 3	SCENARIO 4	SCENARIO 5
Is there a discipline problem?					
If so, who is exhibiting the discipline problem?					
What, if any, is the disruptive behavior?					

Now compare your answers in table 1.1 with our viewpoint. In scenario #1 there is no discipline problem. Carla's behavior is not disrupting the right to learn of any other student so the teacher has decided to ignore it for the time being. She ignores the behavior so that she does not disrupt the flow of the lesson and interfere with the learning of the other students in her class. She thinks that if she ignores Carla's behavior, Carla eventually will catch up with what the rest of the class is doing. She also knows that if the ignoring does not work, she has many other strategies which she can use that will likely bring Carla back on-task while at the same time not be disruptive to the other students. At this time some of you may be thinking, "I couldn't ignore Carla's behavior; soon all the students would be playing with rubber bands." We suggest that since Carla's behavior is not disrupting the rights of others to learn, the teacher, for the time being, continue to ignore it. Carla's behavior may be addressed at a later time and not at the expense of the rest of the students' learning. The fear of others joining in is a legitimate one, but it has been our experience that this rarely occurs on a large scale. Also the probability of it occurring is significantly reduced if the teacher uses techniques that do not draw attention to Carla's behavior.

The second scenario describes a discipline problem, but you may be surprised to learn that the person who is exhibiting the disruptive behavior is the teacher, not Carla. As in the first scenario, Carla's behavior is not interfering with the rights of other students to learn. However, in this case the teacher chooses to immediately confront Carla with a technique that not only draws attention to Carla, but also disrupts the entire class. Because the teacher chooses a technique that interrupts the lesson and reduces the learning time of the other students, the teacher is the discipline problem. In addition, by publicly calling attention to Carla and challenging her with, "we will not continue until . . .," she has also increased the likelihood that Carla will become confrontational in order to show off or "save face" in front of her peers.

You may be having thoughts similar to those of many of the teachers who attend our workshops. For example, you may be thinking, "Sure, Carla isn't disrupting other students, but she is surely interfering with her own learning. I just can't sit idly by and let that happen. She isn't doing what the rest of the class is doing; therefore she is a discipline problem." We believe that every student, including Carla, has the right to choose how to behave, even if the chosen behavior may result in academic failure. What students do not have the right to do is to choose a behavior that interferes with another student's right to learn. Since Carla's behavior is not interfering with anyone's learning but her own, her behavior is not a discipline problem.

Carla's behavior is, however, problematic. The behavior raises a valid issue. What is the difference between a discipline problem and all the other problems that occur in classrooms? Urgency! Discipline problems, because of their effect on others, need immediate teacher attention. When a problem is identified as a non-discipline problem, the teacher has a much wider variety of options involving when and where to intervene. In scenario #2, the teacher must concern herself with the rest of the students' right to learn before addressing Carla's behavior. As you will learn throughout this book, there are many teacher behaviors which simultaneously engage the class in learning activities and also are likely to bring the Carlas of the world back on-task. Such a behavior is illustrated in scenario #3. The teacher involves the class in the homework review while moving next to Carla, influencing her to resume on-task behavior.

There are no discipline problems in scenario #3. As before, Carla's behavior is interfering only with her learning and not the learning of the other students in the class. Unlike scenario #2, where the teacher stops the lesson and challenges Carla, here the teacher chooses a management strategy that does not disturb the other students and at the same time increases the likelihood that Carla will stop playing with the rubber bands and begin to display more on-task behavior. Thus, the teacher avoids becoming a discipline problem.

The fourth scenario presents two persons exhibiting discipline problems. Carla is shooting wads of paper at other students. Her behavior is directly interfering with some of her classmates' learning and is potentially dangerous. The teacher has decided inappropriately to ignore the rubber band shooting. Because the teacher has ignored Carla's interference with the other students' learning, the teacher herself has indirectly interfered with the learning of others. Therefore, she is also a discipline problem.

Scenario #5 illustrates a case where Carla displays a behavior that is a discipline problem for the same reasons as in scenario #4, but the teacher is not a discipline problem. Her choice of behaviors, eye contact, moving close to Carla, and finally talking privately to her, draws as little attention as possible. At the same time, the teacher's behaviors increase the likelihood that Carla will stop shooting paper around the room.

So far our definition of a discipline problem includes any behavior that interferes with the rights of others to learn, is physically or, we would add, psychologically injurious to another person. Furthermore, it has been shown that it is important for teachers not to become a discipline problem themselves. If a student's behavior is a discipline problem and the teacher does not intervene in an appropriate manner, then the teacher is a discipline problem, as illustrated in scenario #4. The teacher is also a discipline problem, whether or not the student's behavior is a discipline problem, if the teacher intervenes in a manner that disrupts the learning of the other students, as in scenario #2.

In the above analyses, discipline problems were attributed to students and/or teachers. We are all very good at describing student behaviors that are discipline problems, but many common teacher behaviors are also discipline problems because of their interference with students' right to learn. For example, teacher behaviors such as coming late to class, ending class early, being unprepared for class, neglecting to consider motivational concerns in lesson planning, all may cause interference with students' right to learn. Parents, classroom aids, or administrators also may exhibit discipline problems if their behavior interferes with the learning rights of students. It is not too difficult for teachers to generate a long list of administrative and parental behavior that may be considered discipline problems.

Finally, two additional behaviors need to be added to arrive at our definition of a discipline problem. The first is any behavior that interferes with the teacher's ability to teach. When a behavior hinders a teacher's effectiveness, it is also interfering with the rights of students to learn. We are not referring here to idiosyncratic annoyances such as the failure of students to sit correctly in their seats or having all desks in straight rows, but rather to serious student misbehavior which objectively could be said to interfere with any reasonable teacher's concentration and focus. These behaviors might include threats to the teacher, comments about the teacher's appearance, ethnic or racial origin.

Secondly, any behavior that destroys property belonging to the school or another student is also considered a discipline problem. This is because students are members of a learning community. The destruction of property belonging to either the community or to individuals seriously threatens the emotional safety of the community members and therefore interferes with the learning process.

Thus the complete definition of a discipline problem is any behavior that 1) interferes with the rights of others to learn, 2) interferes with the ability of the teacher to teach, 3) is physically or psychologically unsafe, or 4) destroys property (Levin and Nolan, 1996).

The importance of this definition is twofold. First, it enables a teacher quickly to identify a discipline problem and differentiate it from other problems that commonly exist in a classroom. By doing so the teacher can more effectively decide when and how to modify her behavior to manage the problem (see Chapters 7, 8, and 9 for detailed discussions on management techniques). Secondly, it provides teachers with a set of behavioral criteria to insure that they never become the discipline problem.

SUMMARY

In this chapter the philosophical underpinnings of this book were explained:

1. There is nothing vastly different in instruction and management that you need to do with disruptive students including those with ADHD. You just have to do it better.
2. The only person you can control is yourself.
3. If you continue to do what you're doing, you'll continue to get what you got.
4. If you can't change your mind, then you can't change anything.
5. Many times, what the teacher is experiencing on an affective level is also what the student experiences.
6. We do not have a responsibility for students, we have a responsibility to students.

Definitions of learning, teaching, and discipline problems were developed.

1. Learning is an observable change in any behavior whether academic, affective, social, or psychomotor.
2. Teaching is the use of preplanned behaviors, founded in learning principles and child development theory and directed toward both instructional delivery and classroom management, which increases the probability of affecting a positive change in student behavior.
3. A discipline problem is any behavior that interferes with the rights of others to learn, interferes with the ability of the teacher to teach, is physically or psychologically unsafe, or destroys property.

Concept Map

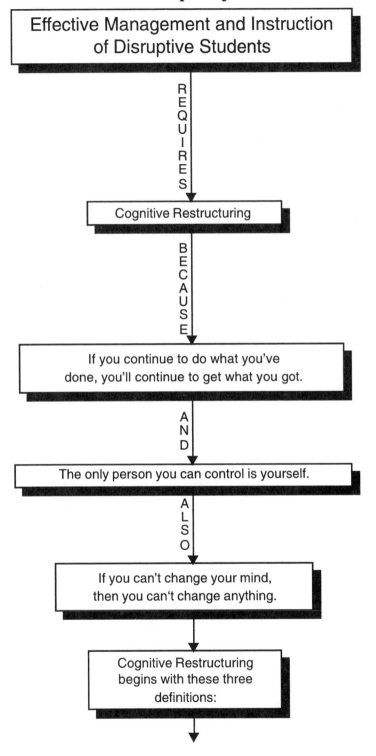

Effective Management and Instruction
of Disruptive Students

REQUIRES

Cognitive Restructuring

BECAUSE

If you continue to do what you've
done, you'll continue to get what you got.

AND

The only person you can control is yourself.

ALSO

If you can't change your mind,
then you can't change anything.

Cognitive Restructuring
begins with these three
definitions:

Learning
An observable change in any behavior whether academic, affective, social, or psychomotor

Teaching
The use of preplanned behaviors, founded in learning principles and child development theory and directed toward both instructional delivery and classroom management, which increases the probability of affecting a positive change in student behavior

Discipline Problem
Any behavior that interferes with the rights of others to learn, interferes with the ability of the teacher to teach, is physically or psychologically unsafe, or destroys property

To increase instructional and management effectiveness keep in mind:

There is nothing vastly different in instruction and management that you need to do with disruptive students. You just have to do it better.

The Parallel Process
Many times what the teacher experiences affectively is also what the student experiences.

REFERENCES

Brendtro, L. K., Brokenleg, M., & VanBocken, S. (1990). *Reclaiming Youth at Risk, Our Hope for the Future*. Bloomington, IN: National Education Service.

Brophy, J. (1988). Research on Teacher Effects: Uses and Abuses. *The Elementary School Journal, 89*, 1, 3-21.

Ginott, H. (1972). *Between Teacher and Child*. New York, NY: Peter H. Wyden Publishing.

Levin, J. and Nolan, J. (1996). *Principles of Classroom Management: A Profession Decision Making Model, 2nd ed*. Needham Heights, MA: Allyn & Bacon.

FREQUENTLY ASKED QUESTIONS

1. What defines excellent teaching?

2. Is it really possible to control one's behavior all of the time?

3. Where should I draw the line for appropriate student behavior when my own beliefs are not congruent with the school code?

4. Which comes first, changes in behavior or attitudes?

5. How can you tell if the teacher is being a discipline problem?

6. You talk about the parallel process; however how can I tell if a student is really feeling the same things I'm feeling, or just pretending?

Chapter 2

Understanding the Behavior of Students with ADHD

INTRODUCTION

Although this text is meant to increase your effectiveness with all students in your classroom, we recognize that students with ADHD form a particular subset whose behavioral problems cause significant difficulties for the classroom teacher. Even if you do not presently have students in your class with ADHD, or you have some philosophical misgivings about students being diagnosed and labeled with the disorder, we encourage you to read this chapter. Students with ADHD are impulsive and frequently act out. There are many students who are not diagnosed with ADHD who also are impulsive and frequently act out and they present similar challenges to the classroom teacher. An understanding of students with ADHD therefore may enhance your effectiveness with these students as well.

Describe to any third grader what the symptoms of ADHD are and he will make the diagnosis for you, "Oh, that's Mickey." Teachers also can readily pinpoint the students who exhibit these symptoms. The symptoms of ADHD cause students, like Mickey, who have the disorder to stand out. (This is emphatically not the case for the subset of students who are diagnosed as ADHD inattentive type. Students whose primary problem is inattention appear to be more spacey than disruptive. This book is about effectively intervening with students who are disruptive. Inattention does not fit our definition of a discipline problem as developed in Chapter 1.)

What becomes problematic is when children seem to have the symptoms of ADHD but, in fact, have other disruptive behavioral disorders and/or depression, anxiety, or any of a host of physiological, psychological, and emotional disorders.

Mickey is a nine year old in third grade. His teacher, Mr. Berk, describes him as a boy who can't seem to sit still. Always in motion, he causes an uproar both intentionally and unintentionally in the classroom. Mickey seems to act as if rules are meant for other people but not for him. This apparent disregard for the norms of behavior causes Mickey to have many difficult interactions both with his peers and with Mr. Berk. Looking into his desk or his Trapper/Keeper is a nightmarish experience which is not for the faint of heart. Old scrunched up papers compete for room with pieces of partially eaten food, broken pencils and crayons, large dead insects connected together by hardened paste, and an assortment of green plastic army figures. To claim that Mickey is disorganized is an understatement on par with claiming that the Grand Canyon is a nice hole. Although it seems that Mickey would like to do well, agreements with Mr. Berk are kept for only ten minutes or so. When consequences are administered, they are greeted with a disbelief and level of emotional upset that causes Mr. Berk to feel like a bully.

Mr. Berk reports that Mickey may be very intelligent, but he also reports being very frustrated because Mickey just doesn't seem to try. What's amazing about Mickey is that in spite of repeated negative interactions which obviously upset him, he continually bounces back with enthusiasm. It's as if all of the bad stuff that happened yesterday doesn't really matter because:

"IT'S NICE OUTSIDE! CAN WE GO OUT? CAN WE HAVE CLASS OUTSIDE? WHY NOT? I WANT TO HAVE CLASS OUTSIDE! EVERYBODY WHO WANTS TO HAVE CLASS OUTSIDE RAISE YOUR HAND! IF I SIT DOWN CAN WE GO OUTSIDE? WHY DO I HAVE TO LEAVE THE ROOM? I DIDN'T DO ANYTHING! LOOK I'M SITTING DOWN. NO, I DON'T WANT TO GO TO THE PRINCIPAL'S OFFICE! WHY ARE YOU ALWAYS PICKING ON ME? I SAID I'M SORRY! I HATE YOU!"

Upon returning from the principal's office, Mickey is able to quickly forget about the negative exchange with Mr. Berk and rapidly immerses himself in whatever he finds interesting at the moment. Unfortunately this may or may not be Mr. Berk's lesson.

So now you have an example of an impulsive, acting out student with ADHD. However, as discussed in Chapter 1, the particular disorder or symptom cluster is not of utmost importance in the design of effective classroom management. As an expert instructional and management professional, you can effectively reach all students except those with the most severe disruptive behaviors. Nevertheless, it is important for teachers to have as part of their knowledge base information regarding the identification and diagnosis of students with ADHD. This knowledge helps teachers to understand these students better, to develop empathy for them, and to form appropriate expectations of these students. Lastly, this knowledge helps teachers avoid becoming frustrated themselves.

An important piece of information is knowing if disruptive behavior is the result of a neurological disorder such as ADHD and therefore possibly unintentional (or more technically, non-volitional), or if the behavior is non-compliant and intentional (or volitional), in order for teachers to have appropriate expectations. Note however, our belief that each human being is responsible for his or her behavior, whether volitional or non-volitional. Some readers may be saying at this point, "But students with ADHD are sometimes unable to control themselves. How can we hold them responsible?" To this we reply, neurology is a mitigating circumstance, not a "get out of jail free card." "The classification of ADD or ADHD is not a license to get away with anything, but rather an explanation that will lead to legitimate help" (Smelter et al., 1996). All students, in order to be part of the general school population, must learn to be responsible for their behavior. It might take more time and effort for students with ADHD, but we do them no favor if we suggest that they are incapable of learning self-control. There are some students with ADHD whom we cannot hold accountable, but these students are not part of the general school population since they comprise a portion of the 20 percent of students with ADHD who cannot be educated effectively in the regular classroom (Kauffman et al., 1995).

Other readers might be thinking, "This ADHD is so over-diagnosed," or how "Everybody is a special needs student nowadays," or that "I have students who behave just like this but they are not diagnosed; what about them?" Whether or not these statements have validity, there are students in your classroom whose behavior is chronically disruptive. Therefore, for the classroom teacher, concerns about over-diagnosis, lack of diagnosis, or the abundance of students with special needs are not significant issues. What is significant is that, "If it quacks like a duck and waddles like a duck, it's a duck." Whether or not Mickey is diagnosed with ADHD or otherwise classified, he is a student who exhibits chronically disruptive behavior which you need to understand and manage. Therefore, what is most necessary is that you make reality your friend and find solutions to the very real problem of effectively teaching every student in your classroom. Now, let's take a closer look at the diagnosis of ADHD and the behavior associated with it.

ADHD SYMPTOMS

Most experts agree that approximately three to nine percent of the general population meets the criteria for ADHD (Szatzmari, et al. 1989; Barkley, 1990). What this means to the classroom teacher is he can expect to see one to three students in most classes with this diagnosis. Of course there may be classes where no students have the disorder, just as there may be classes with four or five students with ADHD.

Boys are far more likely, by a factor of three to one, to be diagnosed (Barkley, 1990). However, there is an increasingly large group of girls who are being diagnosed, particularly since the Diagnostic Statistical Manual IV (DSM IV) was released by the American Psychiatric Association (APA) in 1994 with revised criteria for ADHD, with it's expanded symptom clusters.

All students show a tremendous variation in behavior when compared to some hypothesized norm. It is when this variation significantly impairs performance at home, at school, or with peers that a problem exists. Each of the symptoms of ADHD presented below sometimes is present in the behavior of all students in varying degrees. In order for a student to be diagnosed as having ADHD however, these symptoms must persist across the three domains mentioned above and must significantly impair behavior.

The generally accepted criteria for diagnosis is that a child's symptoms must be more severe and prevalent than what exists for 98 percent of same age students (the 98th percentile), represented by a normative sample group upon which the various behavioral inventories are based (Barkley, 1995a). This equals millions of individuals. Within this population of individuals with ADHD, there exists a continuum which ranges from relatively mild, when compared to others with the disorder or just enough to make the diagnosis, to severely impaired.

Before we delineate the specific symptoms of ADHD, a cautionary note must be sounded. Students, regardless of whether or not they have diagnosable difficulties, are impacted by a variety of ecological factors. These factors include socio-economic status, previous school experiences, parental behavior, physical characteristics, ethnic background, religious background, race, and all the other variables which make us all so diverse. To place students in a box labeled *ADHD* and then have one set of expectations for all of these students, does a disservice to the individual student by ignoring his unique circumstances and characteristics and limits the teacher's instructional and management effectiveness.

Nevertheless, there are certain things that are true for all students with ADHD. The disorder is believed to be hereditary, and therefore children are born with ADHD; they do not develop it later. ADHD is thought to be the result of problems with activity in certain areas of the brain which control impulsivity, arousal, and sensitivity to rewards and punishments (Zametkin, 1989; Zametkin, et al. 1993). ADHD is not, as alleged by some, the result of poor parenting, TV, MTV, sugar in the diet, environmental allergies, yeast infections, fluorescent lighting, too much caffeine, mom working outside the home, single parent families, poor schools, ethnic, or racial background.

Let's look at some student behavior that teachers frequently encounter in the classroom when working with students with ADHD. There are three core symptoms: 1) inattention, 2) impulsivity, and 3) hyperactivity which provide what has been termed the trinity of ADHD symptoms. There are additional symptoms which teachers anecdotally report as coexisting in many students with ADHD. What follows is a theory which the authors feel best explains not only the three core symptoms, but also those symptoms which teachers anecdotally report. These additional symptoms include lack of attention to detail, lack of motivation, problems with self-esteem, failure to learn from experience, difficulty following rules, and emotional reactivity.

Insensitivity to Time Theory

There is a new theory which the authors believe best explains both the three core and anecdotal behavioral symptoms. Dr. Russell Barkley, a renowned researcher in the field of ADHD, has developed a theory of ADHD building upon the theories of Brownowski (1977), author of *The Ascent of Man*. Brownowski states that what separates human beings from other animals is the ability to hold an event constant in one's mind and to perform operations upon this representation of the event. Humans can mentally store an event, freeze it, replay it, slow it down, speed it up, and project the event into the future and back into the past. These abilities are what give human beings their sense of time and history.

For instance, it might give you pleasure to remember a time in the past when something particularly positive occurred in your life, perhaps your graduation from high school or college, your marriage, or the birth of a child. When you think about this event or replay it, you can speed it up or slow it down or freeze the action. You can mentally modify the event to create different outcomes. The same thing can be done for events that you anticipate happening in the future. Using past experience as your guide, you can imagine different scenarios, and alter them by projecting the memory of past events into the future.

Russell Barkley (1995b) hypothesizes that virtually all the symptoms of ADHD, inattention, impulsivity, hyperactivity, as well as the anecdotal symptoms such as lack of attention to detail and failure to learn from experience, can be explained by an insensitivity to time. In other words, if an individual has difficulty holding an event in his mind and performing operations upon it, Barkley predicts that individual will have difficulty delaying responses, learning from the past, adjusting his behavior to ward off future consequences, and planning for future events. This causes the symptom of impulsivity, the appearance of hyperactivity, and inattentiveness. Let's look at a student in a classroom. Imagine that he is bored and happens to have a rubber band and some paper clips handy. The average student might think back to the last time he or another student shot paper clips in the classroom. Remembering the event and its consequences, he projects himself into the future, imagining that he has just shot some paper clips. He can predict, by matching the past to this future, what consequences will befall him. Using this information, he inhibits his response and does not shoot the paper clips. Because of the hypothesized impairment in just these abilities to store, retrieve, and perform operations upon memory, the student with ADHD has difficulty learning from the past and so is not inhibited from action. This student once again shoots the paper clips and so once again is in trouble.

The reason that Barkley's theory is compelling is because it explains more of the symptoms observed in students with ADHD than competing theories. The scope of this book does not allow for a full analysis of this theory or all of the myriad other theories developed to explain the disorder. We refer the interested reader to Barkley's text, *Attention Deficit Hyperactivity Disorder: A Handbook for Diagnosis and Treatment* for a full description of competing theories and to Barkley's taped address to the National Convention of Ch.A.D.D. (Children and Adults with ADHD), "It's About Time!" (1995), for a further description of this current theory.

Core Symptoms

Inattention

The criteria for ADHD includes a subset of symptoms for the purely attentionally disabled (ADHD primarily inattentive type), that is, students for whom the predominant feature is inattention rather than impulsivity/hyperactivity. While we are not focusing on these students as they are not disruptive problems, nevertheless it must be recognized that the majority of all students with ADHD are at least easily bored. They lose interest rapidly, especially towards repetitive tasks where the relevance and/or outcome is not readily apparent. Because of the ease with which these students lose interest, they frequently attend to extraneous classroom stimuli, such as a fly crawling up the wall or counting the holes in the acoustical tile of the classroom ceiling, and not what the teacher has planned such as spelling or geography. Many teachers have been frustrated by the fact that this inattention is highly variable. It is difficult for Mr. Berk to understand how Mickey can be on-task for thirty minutes while the class builds weather instruments while he cannot devote four consecutive minutes to the practice of long division. What teachers need to realize is that this variability in attention helps to confirm that ADHD is present. Students with the disorder show far more variability in attention than the average student. Nevertheless, teachers continue to think that one good day should guarantee another good day. Teachers are often heard saying to their students, "You did this correctly on Monday and Tuesday. Why can't you do it today?" Popper says that "These are students who do well in school two days in a row, and we hold it against them the rest of their lives" (1990).

The only behavior you control is your own. To the extent that you design lessons which are highly relevant and interesting, you increase the likelihood that all students will be more attentive.

Impulsivity

What has taken place during the last ten years of significant research into the syndrome has been a move away from an attention model, as in attention-deficit, and more to a model of *behavioral disinhibition*. This means that when students with ADHD have an urge to perform some behavior, it is difficult for them to suppress it. Teachers and parents are often heard saying to these students, "If only you would stop and think before you did something, you wouldn't get into so much trouble!"

Students with ADHD seem not to learn from previous experiences and the threat of punishment does not seem to deter them. Research shows us that insensitivity to consequences, acting without thinking, and difficulty learning from experience are all characteristic of the impulsivity of ADHD.

This impulsivity makes students with ADHD appear to be willful and defiant. Assuming that the ADHD student is in fact willful and defiant is harmful. The way you think about a student has a lot to do with how you treat that student. If you believe he is willful and defiant, you may be more likely to become frustrated and impatient and act aggressively towards him. This does not mean that students with ADHD are never willful and defiant. They may or may not be. Many students, for reasons other than ADHD, are willful and defiant. In addition, the experiences that students have with impatient and angry adults is more likely to make them defiant and willful than is the presence of ADHD. This is why it is important that you control your behavior as a teacher.

Students with ADHD have a reduced capability to control their impulsive behavior. As we stated in the introduction to this chapter, we do not subscribe to the belief that students with ADHD are incapable of controlling their behavior. When they are alerted to the problem with their immediate behavior, they can and do bring that behavior under control. The fact that they may have to be alerted many, many times and that they have a reduced capability to learn from the past, is what frustrates teachers. Remember again, the only behavior you control is your own. When you do not act impulsively or out of frustration, you increase the likelihood that students will bring their behavior under control.

Hyperactivity

The newest diagnostic criteria have combined impulsivity and hyperactivity into one cluster, because research failed statistically to show each as a discrete factor (APA, 1994). To the classroom teacher, however, this statistical relatedness is probably meaningless. What is more relevant is the behavior actually observed rather than what the behavior is called. Since it is still widely accepted that impulsivity and hyperactivity are separate types of behavior, we discuss them separately.

Students who are outwardly hyperactive are difficult to miss; they stand out and they seem to be all over the place. They frequently push their way to the front of lines to be first. They are impatient and boisterous. They are always on the move, even when they need to sit still; they shake their feet, play with pencils, doodle, rip paper, and play with anything within reach. They act "as if driven by a motor" (APA, 1994). In contrast, there are many students with ADHD who are not overtly hyperactive. They do not leave their seats or bounce off the walls. Instead, they are internally restless and frequently agitated. This covert hyperactivity is particularly evident in adolescents.

Once again, since the only behavior you control is your own, you can change your behavior and accommodate the hyperactive child's need for activity and gross physical movement. For example, you schedule frequent activities which require movement, choose these students to run errands outside the class, or simply allow students to stand at their desks and stretch. By these changes, you decrease the likelihood that the students' hyperactivity is expressed as disruptive behavior.

Anecdotally Reported Symptoms

Lack of Attention to Detail

These students tend to be *Big Picture* kind of people. The mundane and repetitive are intolerable to them. The core symptoms of ADHD make it extremely difficult to stay with any one task too long. Therefore, the finishing up work and the small detail work of assignments, which often spells the difference between success and failure, is often left undone.

Lack of Motivation

Students with ADHD have all the problems that other students may experience with motivation. Over and beyond these normal difficulties, students with ADHD have an impaired ability to accurately assess outcomes, which is a necessary prerequisite for motivation. For a more in depth discussion of motivation see Chapters 4 and 6.

Problems with Self-Esteem

Self-esteem is, in part, an artifact of cumulative life experiences. It is difficult to feel good about yourself when you meet with continual frustration and defeat. Many students with ADHD experience these feelings in school and in social interactions much more than the average student. Some middle school-aged students with ADHD have sadly reported to the authors that they have never been invited to a birthday party or over to another student's house to play. Self-esteem will be discussed in more detail in Chapters 4 and 6.

Failure to Learn From Experiences

It is frequently noted by teachers and parents that these students make the same mistakes over and over again. It seems that they do not profit or learn from previous experiences. One explanation is that if you are impaired in your ability to compare present events with the past and project into the future, then it is difficult to make adjustments in daily behavior.

Difficulty Following Rules

Because of their impulsivity, students with ADHD often seem to ignore classroom rules. Students, in general, follow rules because they are able to predict both positive and negative outcomes to themselves and/or to the classroom community. As has been stated, students with ADHD are impaired in their ability to accurately make these predictions. Therefore rules often are not seriously considered.

Emotional Reactivity

It is often noted that students with ADHD laugh easily and cry easily. They tend to be quite passionate, at least as youngsters. This may be due to so much of the world catching them by surprise. Going back to Barkley's theory about time, with these students it seems to be always NOW. Therefore, being held accountable for previous transgressions is more upsetting and positive events are more exciting.

ADHD Developmental Course

Now that you know something about the symptoms of ADHD, it is important to learn more about how the disorder manifests itself and how symptoms alter throughout the school years. This knowledge will help you adjust your expectations for students at different grade levels and so increase your effectiveness while decreasing your potential frustration.

Most authorities in the field agree that the presence of behavioral symptoms first appear during early childhood and become more pronounced as demands for organization and self-control mount during the early school years. It now is believed that symptoms of ADHD continue to cause impairment well into adulthood. Early misconceptions about ADHD ending sometime during adolescence were due, in large part, to the fact that the more motoric types of hyperactivity tend to diminish with age.

In addition, although students with ADHD have trouble with social interactions due to impulsivity, they ultimately do learn important social rules, albeit more slowly than do their peers. Anecdotal observations indicate that students with ADHD tend to be about thirty percent behind their peers throughout their lifespan on measures of emotional maturity and social skills (Barkley, 1995a).

This gradual shifting of symptoms and "softening" of the social impairments, led early observers to conclude that the disorder was outgrown. What seems to happen is that as students with ADHD become adolescents, young adults, and then adults, their hyperactivity becomes more and more a type of internal rather than external restlessness. The impulsivity may then be manifested as "risky" behavior with sex, addictive substances, and gambling. Serious problems with time management and organizational skills, including procrastination, difficulty prioritizing projects, problems finishing tasks, and forgetfulness still may remain.

Because most adolescents with ADHD are considerably less mature than their peers and also continue to have time management and organizational problems, teachers expecting age appropriate behaviors are frequently disappointed and frustrated. Accurate knowledge of the developmental course of ADHD can help you reduce your frustrations when working with these students.

Sub-Types

We are including a brief description of the sub-types of ADHD so that you will be able to intelligently interact with other professionals in discussing interventions. The current APA criteria differentiate between 3 sub-types: ADHD Primarily Impulsive/Hyperactive, ADHD Primarily Inattentive, and ADHD Combined type (APA, 1994). The students who are likely to become discipline problems are Impulsive/Hyperactive and Combined type. There is some belief that ADHD Primarily Inattentive type is actually a completely separate disorder. Those of you who can recall the "space cowboys or cowgirls" in your classes, the ones that never bothered anyone and whose name you kept forgetting, probably have seen ADHD Inattentive type close up. You probably therefore can readily understand why these students might be thought not to have the same disorder. There is a strong likelihood that the disorder of ADHD Inattentive type will be split from ADHD and listed as a totally discrete disorder in future editions of the DSM.

Interacting with the Student with ADHD

Due to the neurological nature of the disorder and the fact that improvement in self-control occurs at a much slower pace for these students, teachers, no matter what they try, will be interacting with these students more frequently than with the average student. It is very important, therefore, that teachers differentiate between those problems that are truly discipline problems and require immediate, sometimes public intervention and all the other problems that commonly occur in a classroom which can be dealt with in a more casual and private manner. Teacher choices and self-control will either increase the probability of students with ADHD becoming more cooperative and bringing more of their behavior into appropriate limits, or will decrease this probability and further erode the self-esteem and attachment to the learning process that these students evidence.

It is our observation that teachers who are average with other students are terrible teachers for students with ADHD. There is a fortunate corollary; teachers who are effective with students with ADHD are wonderful teachers for all other students in their class.

SUMMARY

Barkley's theory of insensitivity to time was presented as an explanatory model for the core symptoms as well as frequently observed anecdotal symptoms.

The three core behavioral symptoms of ADHD were explained and include:

1. Inattention
2. Impulsivity
3. Hyperactivity

The anecdotal behavioral symptoms were introduced and include:

1. Lack of attention to detail
2. Lack of motivation
3. Problems with self-esteem
4. Failure to learn from experience
5. Difficulty following rules
6. Emotional reactivity

Information provided on the developmental course and the three sub-types of ADHD stressed that symptoms may lessen and soften but ADHD doesn't go away. Finally, it was emphasized again that teacher expectations and behavior are critical in increasing the likelihood of positive classroom behavior of students with ADHD.

Concept Map

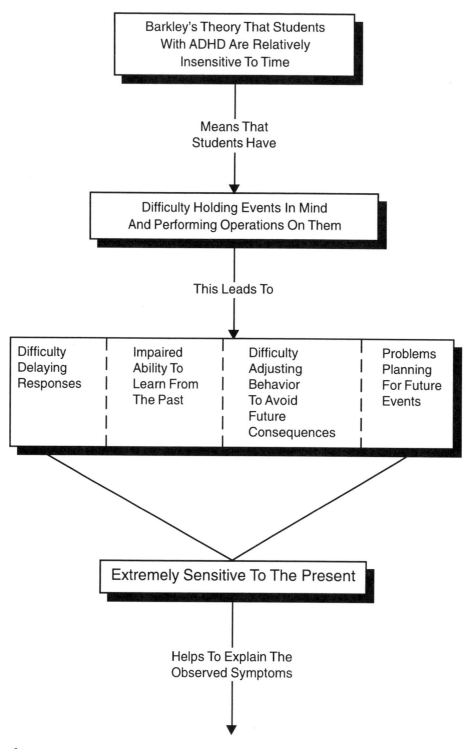

Concept Map

↓

THE ADHD INSENSITIVITY TO TIME CHRONOMETER

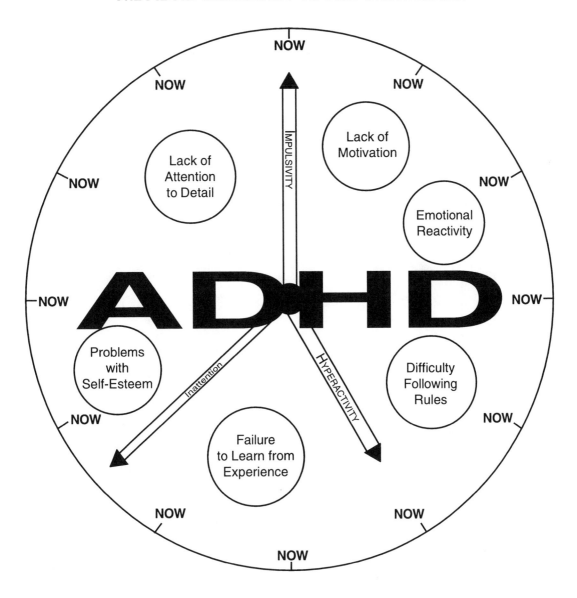

Concept Map

THE SYMPTOMS CLUSTER INTO SUB-TYPES

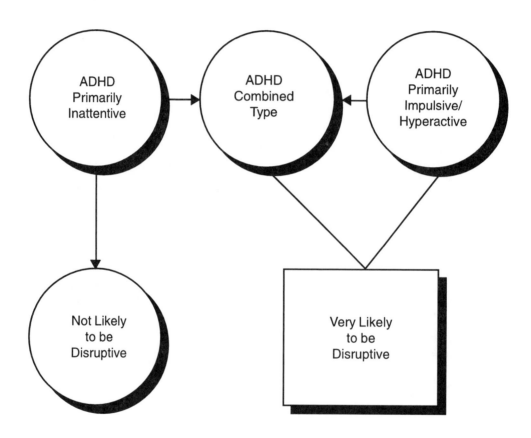

REFERENCES

American Psychiatric Association, (1994). *Diagnostic and Statistical Manual of Mental Disorders,* Fourth Edition. Washington D.C.: American Psychiatric Association.

Barkley, R., (1990). *Attention Deficit Hyperactivity Disorder.* New York: Guilford.

Barkley, R., (1995a). Findings from the cutting edge of research. Address to ChADD 7th Annual Convention, Washington, DC.

Barkley, R., (1995b). *Taking Charge of ADHD.* New York: Guilford.

Brownowski, J., (1977). Human and animal languages. *A Sense of the Future,* pp. 104-131, Cambridge, MA: MIT Press.

Kauffman, J.M., Lloyd, J.W., Baker, J., and Reidel, T.M., (1995). Inclusion of all students with emotional or behavioral disorders? Let's think again. *Phi Delta Kappan,* 76, 7, 542-546.

Popper, K. in Barkley, R., (1990). New ways of looking at ADHD. Address to ChADD 3rd Annual Convention, Washington, DC.

Smelter, R.W., Rasch, B.W., Fleming, J., Nazos, P., Baranowski, S., (1996). Is attention deficit disorder becoming a desired diagnosis?, *Phi Delta Kappan, (77)* 6, 429-432.

Szatzmari, P., Offord, D.R., Boyle, M.H., (1989). Ontario Student Health Study: Prevalence of attention deficit disorder with hyperactivity. *Journal of Student Psychology & Psychiatry & Allied Disciplines,* 30 (2), 219-230.

Zametkin, A.J., (1989). The neurobiology of attention-deficit hyperactivity disorder: A synopsis. *Psychiatric Annals, 19 (11),* 584-586.

Zametkin, A.J., Liebenauer, L.L., Fitzgerald, G.A., King, A.C., et al. (1993). Brain metabolism in teenagers with attention-deficit hyperactivity disorder. *Archives of General Psychiatry,* 50 (5), 333-340.

FREQUENTLY ASKED QUESTIONS

1. Twenty or thirty years ago, we never heard about ADHD. Was it misdiagnosed or is there more of it now?

2. Does the behavior of the student with ADHD affect his grades?

3. Does it work to practice appropriate behaviors with these students, like social skills training?

4. Is it possible for a student diagnosed with ADHD not to show any symptoms in class?

5. Why is it important for me to know which children are diagnosed with ADHD?

6. I have a student who supposedly has ADHD, but he'll work on the computer all day if I let him. How can that be possible?

Chapter 3

Why Students May or May Not Become Discipline Problems: The Influences of Society, Home Life, Student Development, Teacher Behavior

INTRODUCTION

Schools are microcosms of our larger society as has been recognized by educators for over 80 years (Dewey, 1916). The societal climate of the nation, state, city, and the local community significantly influences how students behave in schools.

Parents and educators agree that our society is plagued by drug and alcohol use, crime and violence, child abuse, adolescent suicide, and teenage pregnancy. Therefore, the following statistics may not surprise you (Simons et al, 1991; Children's Defense Fund, 1994).

→ Birth rates among unmarried teenagers are higher now than they have ever been.
→ Almost two-thirds (335,000) of all births to those under age 18 are to unmarried teens.
→ Homicide is the second leading cause of death among people ages 10 to 24.
→ More than 50 percent of seventh to twelfth graders nationwide drink alcohol.
→ More than 2,600,000 children each year are reported abused or neglected.

As these problems have increased, so have the discipline problems in the schools, but clearly these are very complex problems which are only marginally, if at all, affected by teachers and schools.

Student behavior is also an outcome of normal developmental changes. While these changes are not within the control of teachers, they definitely need to be considered in designing effective learning experiences. What is within teachers' control is their instructional competency, which ultimately affects students' behavior in the classroom.

This chapter explores the impact of these various factors on all students, including those with ADHD. However these influences, when superimposed upon the symptoms of ADHD, cause more problems for these students.

THE IMPORTANCE OF UNDERSTANDING
THE INFLUENCES ON STUDENTS' BEHAVIOR

When teachers are asked why they need to understand student misbehavior, they most frequently answer, "so that teachers can arrive at solutions to students' problems." They assume that if they know the causes of a student's disruptive behavior, it is only a matter of time until they arrive at an appropriate solution. If such were the case, the management of disruptive students would be very straightforward; you find the cause and then derive a solution. However, real life is rarely that simple. For example, if you learn that one of your disruptive students is a child who watches five hours of TV a day, comes from an abusive home where the father often is absent, and the child is supervised by his twelve-year-old sister at night when his mother works, what solution do you design? Obviously, there is no easy solution. Even if there were, could it be accomplished by a teacher who works with this student, as well as with thirty other students in school, for approximately thirty hours out of a total of 188 hours a week?

Occasionally knowledge of the causes of a student's disruptive behavior may indeed suggest possible solutions; however, there are two much more important reasons for obtaining this knowledge. These are to avoid negative labeling and to avoid personalizing student behavior.

Avoiding Negative Labeling

Disruptive students are often assigned negative labels. Many of these labels are invented and assigned in faculty rooms. For example, the authors have heard disruptive students called "greasers," "losers," "dumb little _____," and other vulgarities that are not fit to print. More so-called professional labels, but just as damaging, are the "Ten D's of Deviance," including labels of disturbed, delinquent, deprived, dysfunctional, and disobedient (Brendtro, et al., 1990).

Suppose you believe that a disruptive student in your class is an incapable, disrespectful loser; what feelings may you have toward him? Perhaps you feel angry or apathetic. Having these negative emotions, how do you to act toward this student? Possibly, you first try to ignore him. If his behavior continues to be disruptive, you may give him some type of public reprimand or punishment. Such negative teacher behavior is likely to foster similar feelings of anger and apathy in the student. Recall from Chapter 1 that a parallel process such as this one increases the probability that the disruptive behavior will continue.

In contrast, suppose you hold more positive beliefs about this student. You view him as competent but very discouraged. You may then feel interest and concern and use teaching behavior intended to empower and encourage him. These teacher behaviors have a greater likelihood of fostering positive feelings within the student, which in turn decreases the probability of disruptive behavior.

In summary, negative labels result in negative feelings, which in turn result in negative teacher behavior. Positive labels result in positive feelings, which in turn lead to more positive teacher behavior. When teachers are aware of the multitude of influences on students' behavior, they are more likely to develop positive beliefs about the student and avoid negative labels.

Now let's look at the specific label of ADHD. Much good has been done by the hard work of researchers and advocacy groups in getting recognition of the existence of this disorder and the special needs of the population who have it. However, the widespread diagnosis that has followed in the wake of this recognition has engendered a backlash on the part of some segments of the community (The Merrow Report, 1995). Some people have begun to believe that ADHD is over-diagnosed, misdiagnosed and, in fact, some believe the disorder does not even exist. Some people view the diagnosis as an excuse for poor behavior, lack of motivation, lazy work habits, and over-all spoiled kids.

Teachers who share these beliefs probably feel frustrated and angry at the students with ADHD and their parents. Therefore, when a student with the label of ADHD is placed in their class, these teachers are likely to have many negative beliefs which engender negative expectations about future behavior and therefore increase the probability that these problem behaviors will occur.

Teachers who are successful in working with difficult students, including those labeled ADHD, are those who are capable of restructuring their cognitions to foster positive feelings essential for positive actions (Brendtro, et al., 1990). You need to ask yourself whether the label of ADHD sets up in your mind a whole series of negative attributions or it helps to increase your empathy and understanding. Remember, you have a choice.

Avoiding Personalization of Student Behavior

When a teacher works with students who are frequently disruptive, she may allow her professional self-esteem to be directly affected by that student. This is what we refer to as personalization of student behavior. To fully understand the psychology behind this phenomenon, it is necessary to conceptualize what occurs to the teacher's self-esteem when she deals with a frequently disruptive student.

In 1967 Coopersmith conceptualized self-esteem as the sum of a person's perceived significance, competence, virtue, and power; so in setting this up as an equation, we have:

Self-Esteem = Significance + Competence + Virtue + Power

Where:

→ **Significance** is a person's belief that she is respected, liked, and trusted by people who are important to her.
→ **Competence** is a person's sense of mastery of tasks which she values.
→ **Virtue** is a person's perceived feeling of worthiness as a result of her ability and willingness to help others.
→ **Power** is a person's perception that she exerts control over important aspects of her environment.

Because disruptive students are often disrespectful, the teacher might think that this is a result of the students' dislike or distrust of her. This lowers her sense of significance. Because these students often do poorly academically and often disobey the teacher's requests for more appropriate behavior, her sense of competence may decrease. The teacher probably feels that she is not helping the student and so her sense of virtue may also lessen. Therefore, in our self-esteem equation what is left for the teacher to increase in order to feel a greater sense of self-esteem? Power. This is exactly what the teacher uses when she publicly reprimands, humiliates, or punishes the student. The equation now looks like this.

Self-esteem = significance (↓) + competence (↓) + virtue (↓) + POWER (↑)

Ask yourself if you think the teacher's use of power will bring about positive changes in a student's behavior.

Using our formula now to estimate the student's self-esteem, we can make a similar prediction. If a student is publicly reprimanded or humiliated, his sense of significance, competence, and virtue probably is reduced, which leaves him only one means to raise his self-esteem, by increasing his power. Thus the initial misbehavior of the student reduces the teacher's self-esteem, which in turn increases the likelihood of her resorting to power. This decreases the student's self-esteem and increases the probability that the student also will use power, and so on and so on, a vicious cycle to be sure. Once again a parallel process has developed, and the teacher and the student find themselves engaged in the classic no-win power struggle.

Since the only person's behavior you control is your own, you are not forced to react to student power with additional power. You have a choice.

A remarkable example of controlling one's behavior and not reacting to power with power was told to one of the authors by a twelfth grade technology teacher. On the first day of class after mid-year (in this school technology class was a half-year class), a student walked up to this teacher and said, "Let's get something straight right from the beginning. I've got 'til June and I don't want to be hassled. You leave me alone and I'll leave you alone." The teacher chose to ignore the student's remark, but during that week, the teacher noticed that the student was not working. He went up to him and asked about the problem. The student replied, "If you find it necessary to bother me, then I'm going to find it necessary to kick your ass." Rather than react to power with power, the teacher again asked the student to get busy and ignored the student's combative comment. Later that day the teacher tried to find out more about this student. He learned that the student was on the wrestling team. The teacher went to the wrestling meet that week and cheered for the student. The next day the student came into class and said to the teacher that he had seen him at the wrestling match. The teacher replied, "I was a wrestler and I wanted to see how you were doing." The next week the teacher again went to cheer for this student. Then he waited until the student was out of the locker room and congratulated him on a fine match. This was the start of many conversations about wrestling. The teacher reported that this student caused no problems in his class for the rest of the semester. Probably even more important for the student than stopping his disruptive behavior was that during the semester the teacher assisted the student in learning more appropriate ways of using his power than threatening people with bodily harm.

In the above series of events, the teacher refused to enter into a power struggle with the student. The teacher used his professional competence and sense of virtue to change his behavior toward the student. The teacher's demonstration of interest in the student's athletic activity apparently helped the student feel more competent and more significant. Because the student felt increases in two other areas of self-esteem, he no longer needed to demonstrate his power. One of the key points of this anecdote is that a teacher's sense of competence, significance, virtue, and power cannot be predicated upon her students' behavior if she is to be maximally effective as a teacher.

Students with ADHD due to their higher than average need for feedback and stimulation will seek your attention, especially when young, more often than the average student. In addition, these students tend to be more disruptive to the classroom environment than the average student. It is possible that after you have provided positive, consistent feedback to the student and designed motivating lessons, and you find yourself still dealing with the same problem behavior, you may begin to feel that the student is persecuting you. Of course, you probably will feel this way under similar circumstances with any student. What is important to note is that the possibility of this situation occurring with a student with ADHD is much higher than with the average student. Students with ADHD can change their behavior, but will require more patience and understanding on your part than even other highly disruptive students. Remember, no matter what the situation is, personalizing any student behavior decreases your effectiveness.

So now you may be wondering how to retain your professional self-esteem when working with students who frequently are disruptive. The answer is through positive interaction with your professional colleagues, active participation in your professional societies, involvement in professional committees in your school, and continuous study in your discipline and pedagogy. Also you retain your professional self-esteem through the knowledge that you are employing the definition of teaching, which is changing your behavior in ways that increase the likelihood that students will change their behavior in positive ways. Doesn't it make more sense to base your self-esteem on what you can control, on your professional activities and teaching behavior, than on what you can't control, students' behavior and students' self-esteem?

INFLUENCES ON STUDENTS' BEHAVIOR

Television

The average American child spends almost as much time watching television, 23 to 28 hours per week, as he does in the classroom (American Psychological Association, 1993). As a result, television has become the primary source of information for young people. Along with issues about the frequency of sex and portrayal of racial/gender stereotypes on television, researchers are concerned most with the amount of violence depicted.

Content analysis of shows indicates notable differences in television violence during the last forty years. In 1992 there were approximately thirty-two acts of violence per hour in shows watched by children, the highest ever recorded, as compared to only eleven acts of violence per hour in 1950. It is estimated that an average child in the 1990's watches 8,000 televised murders and 100,000 acts of violence before finishing elementary school (Congressional Quarterly, 1993). Violence is not solely seen on fictional television programs, but real-life violence often consumes the majority of the nightly news and prime time news shows.

For decades, research has been conducted on the influence of television violence upon children's behavior. A 1982 National Institute of Mental Health Report, entitled "Television and Behavior: Ten Years of Scientific Progress and Implications for the Eighties," stated that research findings support a causal relationship between television violence and aggressive behavior (Bouthilet and Lazar, 1982). A definitive statement was made by the American Psychological Association: "There is absolutely no doubt that higher levels of viewing violence on television are correlated with increased acceptance of aggressive attitudes and increased aggressive behavior" (1993, p. 33).

It has been hypothesized that television violence influences behavior not only through role modeling aggressive solutions to conflicts (Pearl, 1984), but also by creating the *bystander effect*, the desensitization or callousness toward violence directed at others (Congressional Quarterly, 1993). It has been proposed that violence on television produces stress in children, and that too much exposure to violence, in time may lead to disturbed behavior (Rice, 1981).

To the extent that any child or adolescent is more likely to behave aggressively as the result of the depiction of violence in the media, the individual with ADHD is likely to have greater difficulty inhibiting his behavior because of his impulsivity.

What may actually prove to be more problematic than the passive viewing of television violence is the hands-on, although vicarious, participation in violence required by video games, 80 percent of which contain violence (Congressional Quarterly, 1993).

Knowledge Explosion

Have you surfed the Information Super Highway, otherwise known as the Internet, or visited the World Wide Web lately? If you have, then you have some idea of what is meant by the term *knowledge explosion.* If you haven't, you are in for a real culture shock. The knowledge explosion or information age is considered to have begun in the mid 1950's after the Russians launched Sputnik, the first satellite. The catalyst for this explosion of knowledge was the national fear that the Russians were surpassing us in scientific knowledge and technological advancements.

In the early 1970's, it was estimated that in a 50 year span, from 1980 to 2030, the world's knowledge would increase 32 times representing 97 percent of the world's collective body of knowledge (Toffler, 1970). More recent estimates indicate that this figure might be too low. The technological advances attributed to this knowledge explosion include VCRs, cellular phones, Direct TV, FAX machines, CD-Rom, and powerful personal portable computers. These advances serve to increase the rate of the knowledge explosion by making possible the instantaneous communication of worldwide information.

The knowledge explosion influences students' behavior in three ways. First, for some students, it serves as a mechanism for the erosion of respect for authority. There has always been a generation gap, but now this rapid explosion of knowledge is producing what has been called *generation discontinuities.* By the end of elementary school and definitely by the end of high school, most students possess knowledge that their parents only vaguely comprehend. This is clearly illustrated in the areas of personal computing, telecommunications, environmental science, astronomy, and graphical calculators. Thus respect that was once an attribute of adulthood because of adults' worldliness and expertise has begun to erode.

The erosion of authority is also the result of students being keenly aware of the present state of world affairs. The awareness of famine, terrorism, political corruption, and mass murders is the product of the instantaneous communication technologies which are available today. Therefore, it does not take students much time to begin to view adults as being relatively ineffective in managing their own adult world, yet alone relying upon them for solutions in managing the students' world.

The second reason that the knowledge explosion affects students' behavior is because it affects teachers' behavior. Teachers are being called upon more than ever before to restructure their instruction while keeping abreast of the latest developments in their respective content areas. These expectations are often made without administrators providing adequate release time or training. Concentrating only on pedagogy, teachers are expected to understand and use cooperative education strategies, performance-based assessments, student portfolios, authentic instruction, instructional technologies, strategies that account for multiple intelligences, multicultural curriculum, interdisciplinary units, and more. This is all to be accomplished in the inclusive classroom.

Sounds overwhelming, doesn't it? Teachers constantly tell us that they are indeed overwhelmed and burned out. How does this affect students' behavior? How effective and willing are you to empathize with and be supportive of a student who doesn't understand or can't sit in his seat for the fifth time in two days, when you are stressed, overwhelmed, and burned out? How about if it's a student with ADHD who hasn't been able to sit in his seat for the tenth time today and has asked four times in the last fifteen minutes, "When is recess?" Not very, we suspect. Consider your answer with respect to the definition of teaching, changing your behavior in a way that increases the likelihood that students change their behavior in appropriate ways. It seems clear that it is difficult to make these changes if you are stressed and lack the emotional energy to remain patient and understanding, which is essential in your interactions with difficult children.

The third reason is the direct influence the knowledge explosion has on the curriculum. Students are expected to learn more now, in the same amount of time, than any previous generation. Many curriculums merely add the new material on top of the older material. This requirement of more material causes students to experience higher levels of stress. This stress is often relieved by disruptive behavior or just tuning out. In other districts the curriculum has not caught up with the information explosion or the technologies used to deliver the information. In these schools many students feel that the curriculum does not reflect nor does it relate to what is happening in the real world. Unless important decisions are made about what content is most important to know, and how it most effectively can be delivered, many students will be bored and find their schooling lacking relevancy. What teachers often label as a lack of motivation may actually be their students' inability to feel any direct connection with what is occurring in the classroom (Gaby, 1991). It is only a very small step from lack of relevancy and boredom to disruptive behavior. An understanding of this issue by educators is what supports the restructuring efforts in many schools.

Home Environment

The home life for many children, unfortunately, is more disadvantaged today than it was thirty years ago, and the gap between the rich and the poor has widened every year since 1986 (Coontz, 1995). This is particularly troublesome to educators who, for a long time, have recognized the significant influence of a child's home environment on school behavior and academic progress (Feldhusen et al, 1973; Levine, 1984, Coontz, 1995). Recently, the President of the Elementary School Principals Association, said that there never will be any lasting educational reform until there is parental reform (Whitmire, 1991). In 1993, the American Psychological Association concluded that breakdowns in family processes and relationships are contributing factors to children's antisocial behaviors. Family characteristics that are related to children's antisocial behavior include parental rejection, inconsistent discipline, physically abusive discipline, parental support for their children's use of aggressive conflict resolution approaches, and lack of parental supervision (which is one of the strongest predictors of later conduct problems).

What makes the home life of American children significantly different than in previous decades? Consider some of these additional statistics from the US Bureau of the Census, 1994, Children's Defense Fund, 1994, and Coontz, 1995.

→ Between 1960 and 1993, the divorce rate increased over 100 percent.
→ If the proportion of births to unmarried parents continues, more than 40 percent of all babies born in 2001 will be to single mothers.
→ More than 20 percent of all children live in poverty—more than any year since 1965.
→ Children raised in poverty have a much greater likelihood of experiencing a wide range of problems including, but not limited to, learning and behavior problems, engagement in violent behavior, and unwed parenthood.
→ More than half of single parent families are at or below the poverty level.

Abraham Maslow's (1968) theory of basic human needs provides an explanation as to why problems in a child's home environment are predictive of academic and behavioral problems in school. Maslow proposed that human beings have five basic needs that are met in a hierarchical order. If the lower level needs are not met, then an individual may have difficulty meeting the higher level needs in prosocial ways, if at all. These needs from the lowest level to the highest level are:

→ **Physiological**—the need for nutritious food and a healthy environment
→ **Safety and Security**—the need for a safe, secure environment
→ **Belonging and Affection**—the need for care, love, and respect
→ **Self-Esteem and Respect**—the need for significance, competence, and worthiness
→ **Self-Actualization**—the need to use talents and abilities to experience self-fulfillment

This theory assumes that younger children spend considerably more time and effort in meeting the lower level needs than higher needs, while from preadolescence on, assuming the lower level needs are met, the focus shifts to meeting the higher order needs of self-esteem and self-actualization. Furthermore, the theory suggests that the lower level needs are met best at home, while the higher order needs are met most meaningfully by out-of-home experiences such as school, when children interact with their peers and are expected to use their abilities and talents in accomplishing increasingly complex tasks. Thus if children or adolesecents live in dysfunctional or disadvantaged home environments, the likelihood that they have met their lower level needs is questionable. Therefore, as students they are likely to have difficulty with academic achievement and pro-social behavior, both of which constitute higher order needs.

Children with ADHD experience all of the same problems inherent to the modern family as the average student. In addition, parents of children with ADHD report higher levels of stress and depression and more frequent angry conflicts with their children (Cunningham et al, 1988; Brown and Pacini, 1989). These factors make it more difficult for the parent to have the increased patience and understanding needed to help these children meet their basic needs.

Cognitive and Moral Development

Some disruptive behaviors are outcomes of normal cognitive and moral development. As children move through the various stages of development, they interpret and react to their environment differently than they did at earlier developmental stages. At later stages of development, students question more about anything and everything. Students begin to consider alternative views of issues, and they begin to understand there are a variety of different actions that may be taken in any given situation. Many of these actions or exploratory behaviors are quite disruptive in structured learning environments. Unless the teacher understands these changes and designs learning opportunities that enable students to use and further develop their new found cognitive abilities and moral reasoning in pro-social ways, the possibility of disruptive behavior increases.

The famous developmental psychologist Jean Piaget spent his professional career studying the manner in which children develop cognitively. As you probably know, his work resulted in a four stage cognitive development theory that is somewhat age dependent (1970). The stages are 1) sensori-motor, 2) pre-operational, 3) concrete operations, and 4) formal operations.

There are typical behaviors that are associated with each stage. However, most behavioral problems that arise from cognitive development occur as students move into the fourth and final stage, formal operations. Sometime between twelve and fifteen years of age, adolescents begin to develop the ability to think abstractly and use independent critical thinking skills that include viewing the world differently. These views may not be similar to those espoused by their teachers and parents. This divergence of opinions frequently leads to arguing, testing the limits, and questioning authority. If these students are in highly-structured, teacher-centered classes where independent thought and questioning is discouraged, you can guess what occurs. We have disruptive behavior. Due to the impulsivity and disinhibition of children with ADHD, these types of behaviors will be even more intense and will likely occur with greater frequency.

If teachers understand these behaviors for what they really are, normal cognitive development, and provide learning opportunities that allow these new cognitive abilities to be used in appropriate ways, the behavior is no longer disruptive. For example, classes that involve students in debating, taking and defending a point of view, considering alternatives, and bucking the status quo are rarely plagued by disruptive adolescent behavior.

Lawrence Kohlberg (1969) theorized that children progress through six stages of moral development. The stages are 1) punishment-obedience, 2) exchange of favors, 3) good boy-nice girl, 4) law and order, 5) social contract, and 6) universal ethical. Corresponding with Piaget's cognitive stage of formal operations, are Kohlberg's moral stages of "good boy-nice girl" and "law-order."

In early to mid adolescence when students are in junior and senior high school, they move into the good boy-nice girl orientation, where conformity to peer pressure often dictates behavior. After this, students enter the law and order stage. In the law and order stage, what is right and wrong is delineated within well-defined boundaries. Judgments are made on the basis of somewhat inflexible laws and often these laws of behavior are those of cliques and youth subcultures. Because of the rigid boundaries, students are quick to point out to adults inconsistencies in expected behavior. It is not uncommon to hear students questioning adults such as, "Why do I have to do this and you don't?" or making remarks such as "Don't tell me what to do; I'm capable of taking care of myself," and "What you're asking me to do is really stupid. It makes no sense." Students no longer accept blindly the rationale of "because I said so," and they rebel against "that's the way it is" justifications. Teachers who are unaware of the behavior that accompanies these stages are prone to take students' very poor attitudes and comments as personal attacks on their authority or label them as disrespectful or ungrateful spoiled kids, thus creating a parallel process. It is much more constructive to recognize these behaviors as the inappropriate and unskilled use of students' new way of thinking. Inappropriate or not, it represents normal moral development. By being aware of students' development and the associated types of typical behavior, teachers are able to plan learning activities that provide students with opportunities to challenge the adult world in prosocial ways.

A few students, by the end of high school, may reach the "social contract" stage. In this stage, morality is a function of the protection of individual rights and democratic principles. Motives and individual values are critical in making moral decisions. When these students make their moral decisions, they take into account the reasons behind an individual's action and the individual's values. What behavior may you expect to observe in a student who is moving into the social contract stage in a classroom of a teacher who is most interested in compliant behavior, no matter what? We're sure that you are imagining various types of quite disruptive behavior.

Since cognitive and moral development seem to be interactive and simultaneous processes, teachers must consider both when observing students' behavior. Table 3.1 below presents specific characteristics of the various stages of cognitive and moral development. Take a few minutes to fill in the last column, Common Behaviors. Ask yourself what behaviors are likely to result when the various cognitive and moral stages interact?

TABLE 3.1 *Common Student Behaviors In The Classroom Associated With The Interaction Of Cognitive And Moral Development*

AGE	COGNITIVE/MORAL DEVELOPMENTAL CHARACTERISTICS	COMMON STUDENT BEHAVIORS
2 to 7	–difficulty considering other points of view –egocentric –behaviors dependent upon receiving rewards or punishments	
7 to 12	–limited ability to think abstractly –little concern with inconsistencies in their thinking –early in this stage actions based on reciprocal favors –later in this stage actions based on peer conformity –motives behind other's actions not fully considered	
12 and older	–ability to think abstractly develops –motives behind others' actions are considered –rigid boundaries of acceptable behavior –individuals' rights beginning to be considered	

Hopefully this exercise helps you to recognize that many of the behaviors you observe in your classroom are developmentally appropriate and are normal behaviors. How disruptive they become is highly dependent upon whether or not you accommodate these developmental changes when designing instruction.

With this new view of cognitive and moral development in mind, let's think about our great social leaders, those people whose actions made society a fairer and more just place for all people. People such as Martin Luther King, Susan B. Anthony, Rosa Parks, Mahatma Ghandi, Ceasar Chavez, and Nelson Mandella, as well as many others, may come to mind. At what stages of development do you think they were? Next ask yourself, "What common behaviors did they exhibit?" Upon reflection, you may be struck by the fact that they all broke the law. They all challenged authority. They all were very disruptive. What does this tell you?

Instructional Behavior

Think of the best teacher that you have ever had, the teacher that you would like to model yourself after, the one of whom you have fond memories. Now think about the worst teacher you ever had, the one that you never wanted to be like. Compare these two teachers' personal and professional characteristics. To help you compare, take a moment and fill in Table 3.2.

TABLE 3.2 *Comparisons Between Best And Worst Teacher*

QUESTION	BEST TEACHER	WORST TEACHER
What words do you use to describe this teacher?		
How do you think this teacher felt about you?		
How did you feel about the teacher?		
When you experienced problems, did you feel comfortable approaching this teacher?		
Did students desire to behave in this teacher's class or were they afraid to misbehave?		
Were there a lot of students off task and disinterested in this class?		
Were there a lot of students misbehaving in this class?		
Did you understand the material that this teacher was teaching?		
Were you willing to ask for help when you didn't understand the material?		
Did the teacher communicate support and a willingness to help you and the other students?		
Was this teacher's instruction organized and easy to follow?		
Did the teacher try to relate the material to your experiences and your interests?		
Did this teacher communicate a real interest in you?		
Did you learn a lot in this teacher's classroom?		
Did it appear to you that this teacher enjoyed teaching?		

From your answers, it probably is evident that you have very different perceptions and feelings for your best and your worst teacher. Furthermore, if you are similar to the thousands of teachers to whom we have asked these same questions, there were probably many more off-task, uninterested, disruptive students in your worst teacher's class than in your best teacher's class.

Just as the two teachers you described affected the behavior of their students, your instructional competence also influences your students' behavior. Therefore, instructional competence or incompetence is an influence just like television, knowledge explosion, home environment, and cognitive and moral development. However, there is a very significant difference between your behavior and the other influences on student behavior that have been discussed. You have very little, if any, control over the media or student home environment. You also exert little control over the influences of the knowledge explosion and the cognitive and moral development of a student in your classroom, although your knowledge of these influences has significant implications for the types of learning experiences which you design. In contrast, you do have total control of your own behavior in a classroom, including your interpersonal and instructional behavior. By ensuring and continually increasing your instructional competence, you are ameliorating the effects of negative outside influences as well as preventing the misbehavior that occurs as a direct result of poor instruction (Levin and Nolan, 1996).

To your students, instructional competence translates into your ability to explain and clarify the material so that they understand it. Your ability to present lessons clearly, so that students understand and succeed, increases the likelihood that your students will "like you" (Kounin, 1970). Look back at Table 3.2. It is very probable that you wrote that you "liked" your best teacher and "disliked" your worst teacher. This is important because Kounin (1970) found that students are more motivated to behave appropriately in classes where they like the teacher. Upon further investigation, Kounin noted that the disliked teachers were those who lacked instructional clarity and left students with some degree of confusion, which inevitably led to disruptive behavior.

The relationship between instructional competence and student behavior is clearly evident in the following two classrooms, located in the same school district (Levin and Nolan, 1996).

Ms. Doughterty taught mathematics in a suburban school district. Her classes were plagued by disruptive behavior. The misbehavior was so frequent that it attracted the attention of the principal. Students were continually moving throughout the room, calling out, throwing paper, talking, and occasionally openly confrontational to Ms. Dougherty when she requested appropriate behavior. One of the authors interviewed the students, who provided the following comments about Ms. Dougherty's teaching.

1. She gave unclear directions.
2. Topics that she discussed were not related to the subject matter.
3. She repeated material which was already understood.
4. She wrote sloppily on the board and did not explain what she wrote.
5. When we asked for help, she often answered, "we already did that."
6. She always called on the same people to answer.
7. She gave answers to our questions that we couldn't understand.
8. She didn't explain how we could use the material.
9. She always used note cards.
10. She told us that she could not understand why the class was having difficulty.
11. She didn't go over homework.

In stark contrast to Ms. Dougherty's teaching is that of Ms. Cuervo. Ms. Cuervo taught fifth grade. Her students expressed sorrow over the fact that school would soon be ending for summer vacation. During the interviews of her students, they also made comments about her.

1. We can give our opinions.
2. She doesn't say anything to us if we say something stupid.
3. She lets us decide how we will do things.
4. She makes suggestions and helps us when we get stuck.
5. We are allowed to say how we feel.
6. We have choices.
7. We don't have to think like her.
8. We learn a lot.

The comments made by the students about each teacher are very revealing. They all pertain to instructional factors that are completely in the control of the teacher. Ms. Dougherty's behavior increased the likelihood that her students were disruptive, which indeed they were. Ms. Cuervo's behavior increased the likelihood that her students were on-task and engaged in learning to the point that they were sorry that school would soon end. This illustrates how the definition of teaching, changing your behavior in a manner that increases the likelihood that students will change their behavior, occurs in the real world.

Once again we stress that the only person who you can control is yourself. There are many factors outside of your control which influence student behavior. However, if you conceptualize the management of student behavior as a function of curriculum, instruction, and classroom climate, which you can control, you are more likely to be successful than if you perceive management as a function of your role as an authoritarian or disciplinarian (Duke, 1982; Brophy, 1988). The choice is yours to design effective learning environments or become a disciplinarian.

The authors have found that almost every student having ADHD has had at least one teacher who has had relatively little or no difficulty with him. It is our belief, which we shall expand upon in later chapters, that instructional competence combined with effective classroom management skills and a respectful attitude is what characterizes each of these relationships. Students try harder and behave better for people they believe like them and who can reach them both cognitively and emotionally. Your mission, should you decide to accept it, is to become that teacher. Remember, teachers who are effective for children with ADHD are wonderful teachers for all other children in their class.

SUMMARY

This chapter explained the importance of understanding the influences on childrens' behavior. With this understanding, teachers decrease the likelihood that they will label students or personalize students' behavior, thus increasing their effectiveness in managing disruptive behavior. The dynamics of negative labels and how these lead to negative teacher behavior was described. Self-esteem was defined as the sum of significance, competence, virtue, and power. Self-esteem was used to define what is meant by the personalization of student behavior, and the personalization of student behavior was then used to illustrate how a parallel process develops.

Several influences on students' behavior were explored. These were 1) television, 2) knowledge explosion, 3) home environment, 4) cognitive and moral development, and 5) instructional behavior. It was stressed that, of these influences, the only one under the direct control of the teacher is instructional competence. These influences were further analyzed as to their stronger impact upon the student with ADHD.

Concept Map

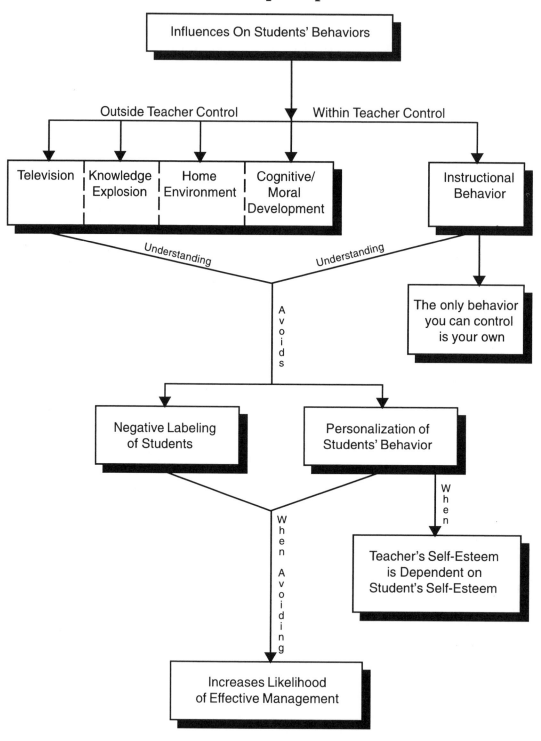

REFERENCES

American Psychological Association. (1993). *Violence and Youth: Psychology's Response,* Vol. 1., Washington, DC: American Psychological Association.

Bouthilet, P. D., and Lazar, J. (Eds.). (1982). *Television and Behavior: Ten Years of Scientific Progress and Implications for the Eighties.* U.S. Department of Health and Human Services, National Institute of Mental Health, Washington, DC: U.S. Government Printing Office.

Brendtro, L. K., Brockenleg, M., & VanBocken, S. (1990). *Reclaiming Youth at Risk, Our Hope for the Future.* Bloomington, IN: National Education Service.

Brophy, J. (1988). Educating teachers about managing classrooms and students. *Teaching and Teacher Education, 4,* 1, 1-18.

Brown, R. T. and Pacini, J. N. (1989). Perceived family functioning, marital status, and depression in parents of boys with attention deficit hyperactivity disorder. *Journal of Learning Disabilities, 22,* 9, 581-587.

Congressional Quarterly. (1993). TV violence. *CQ Researcher, 3,* 12, 165-187.

Children's Defense Fund. (1994). *State of America's Children, Yearbook 1994.* Washington, DC: Children's Defense Fund.

Coontz, S.(1995). The American family and the nostalgia. *Phi Delta Kappan, 76,* 7, K1-K20.

Coopersmith, S. (1967). *The Antecedents of Self Esteem.* San Francisco, CA: W.H. Freedman.

Cunningham, C. E., Benness, B. B., Siegel, L. S. (1988). Family functioning, time allocation, and parental depression in the families of normal and ADHD children. *Journal of Clinical Child Psychology, 17,* 2, 169-177.

Dewey, J. (1916). *Democracy and Education.* New York: Macmillan.

Duke, D. L. (1982). *Helping Teachers Manage Classrooms.* Alexandria, VA: Association for Supervision and Curriculum Development.

Feldhusen, J. F., Thuroton, J. R., and Benning, J. J. (1973). A longitudinal study of delinquency and other aspects of children's behavior. *International Journal of Criminology and Penology, 1,* 341-351.

Gaby, J. (1991). *ASCD Update,* Jan.

Kohlberg, L. (1969). *Stages in the Development of Moral Thought and Action,* New York, NY: Holt, Rinehart & Winston.

Kounin, J. S. (1970). *Discipline and Group Management in Classrooms.* New York: Holt, Rinehart & Winston.

Levin, J. and Nolan, J. F. (1996). *Principles of Classroom Management: A Professional Decision Making Model,* second ed. Needham Heights, Allyn & Bacon.

Levine, V. (1984, August). Time use and student achievement: A critical assessment of the National Commission Report. *Forum* (College of Education, The Pennsylvania state University), *11,* 12.

Maslow, A. (1968). *Toward a Psychology of Being.* New York: D. Van Nostrand.

The Merrow Report, Attention Deficit Disorder: A Dubious Diagnosis. (1995). Public Broadcasting Service.

Pearl, D. (1984). Violence and aggression. *Society, 21,* 6, 15-16.

Pearl, D., Bouthilet, L., and Lazar, J. (Eds.). (1982). *Television and Behavior: Ten Years of Scientific Progress and Implications for the Eighties.* Vol. 2., U.S. Department of Health and Human Services, National Institute of Mental Health, Washington, DC: U.S. Government Printing Office.

Piaget, J. (1970). Piaget's Theory, In P. H. Mussen (Ed.) Carmichael's *Manual of Child Psychology,* Vol. 1. New York, NY: Wiley.

Rice, P. F. (1981). *The Adolescent Development, Relationships, and Culture,* 3rd ed. Boston, MA: Allyn & Bacon.

Simons J. M., Finlay, B., and Yang, A. (1991). *The Adolescent and Young Adult Fact Book.* Washington, DC: The Children's Defense Fund.

Toffler, A. (1970). *Future Shock.* New York, NY: Random House.

U.S. Bureau of the Census. (1994). *Statistical Abstract of the United States, 1994.* Washington, DC: U.S. Government Printing Office.

Whitmire, R., (1991). Educational declines linked with erosion of family. *The Olympian,1,* Oct.

FREQUENTLY ASKED QUESTIONS

1. It was stated that a discipline problem is when a behavior interferes with the rights of others to learn. So refusing to work is not a discipline problem. But what if refusing to work continues? It doesn't disrupt the class, but slowly it influences some other students and they start saying, "He's not doing anything. Why do I have to?" Does the refusal to work then become a discipline problem?

2. How can we not take misbehavior personally?

3. It was stated that as students develop cognitively and morally they become more disruptive. I thought that students become easier to manage as they get older. How can this be?

4. How involved should a teacher be with students' problems that result from poverty, abuse, or divorce. Should we intervene, inquire, seek help, or is there a professional boundary that teachers should not cross?

5. Will controlling one's behavior really overcome the majority of problems that students bring with them to the classroom?

6. Are there ways to keep from taking something a student says or does personally, especially when the student means it?

7. If teachers are to base their lessons according to the cognitive stages of their students, what happens when there are students at different stages in the same classroom?

Chapter 4

Why Students May or May Not Become Discipline Problems: Students' Success/Failure Ratio, Motivation, Self-Esteem

INTRODUCTION

"Gee Officer Krupke, You've done it again.
These boys don't need a job; they need a year in the Pen.
It ain't just a question of misunderstood;
deep down inside them they're no good!"

These sentiments, first expressed in the late 1950's in the musical West Side Story, are echoed today by many teachers, citizens, and lawmakers. Is it true? Are disruptive students inherently "no good?" We don't think so.

Certainly it seems that disruptive students are discouraged and defeated, at least by the time of adolescence. They no longer seem to care what teachers and other authority figures think about them. These students seem to gravitate towards groups that condone and encourage negative behavior. In classes and at home, they show a lack of motivation that can be frustrating and even infuriating to the concerned teacher and parent.

Instead of giving up on these students and labeling them "no good," in this chapter we continue to look at the reasons for their behavior. In addition to those influences which you studied in the last chapter including television violence, knowledge explosion, home environment, cognitive and moral development, and teacher instructional behavior, this chapter analyzes students' behavior in terms of three inter-related concepts which concern the student herself: 1) success/failure ratio, 2) motivation, and 3) self-esteem. We explain how the three concepts are important in understanding why students may or may not become behavioral problems.

THE SUCCESS/FAILURE RATIO

An individual's self-worth is, in large part, determined by the ratio of her successes (S) to her failures (F) or S/F (Gever, 1991). In order for an individual to have a reasonably good opinion of herself, this ratio must be greater than 1. In other words, she must experience more success experiences than failure experiences in life. We denote this as S/F > 1. This is not to say that a person who experiences 200 successes and 199 failures, or the $S/F = 200/199 = 1.005$, feels as positive about herself as an individual who experiences 400 successes and 199 failures or the $S/F = 400/199 = 2.01$. What we mean when we use the shorthand notation $S/F > 1$, is that the person has many more successes than failure experiences in life. This concept was first proposed over one hundred years ago (James, 1890) but to the best of the authors' knowledge, its application to understanding students' disruptive behavior has gone relatively unnoticed (Gever, 1982).

Human beings are social animals who have an innate desire to belong, be recognized, and accepted (Adler, 1963). When we speak of success, we are not speaking only of winning the contest or earning the highest grade in the exam. We mean that the student receives feedback from her environment which meets her needs to belong, be recognized, and be accepted. Examples of success outside of school include each time her mom or dad expresses positive regard toward her, each time her friends include her in activities, or each time she accepts and successfully accomplishes her responsibilities. In school, success may include receiving high or even passing grades, contributing to classroom activities, having fun during recess, or enjoying lunchtime with her friends. Throughout many students' lives, their successes greatly outnumber their failures. Of course all students have bad days and experiences. Sometimes the difficulty of an exam takes them by surprise and they fail. Sometimes the conversation that the student had in the schoolyard just has to be continued in class, leading to a negative interaction with the teacher. Sometimes friends are fickle and suddenly may exclude the student. Occasionally Mom or Dad is in a bad humor and takes it out on the student. Each of these may be perceived as a failure experience for the individual student. However for the average student, the total number of successes still greatly outnumber the failures, leaving S/F ratio greater than 1. The stockpile of success experiences that the average student compiles in the course of her life inoculates her against even relatively prolonged periods of failure which might stem from factors such as parental discord, divorce, personal or family illness, one or two poor terms of schoolwork, or some setbacks in social situations.

Students with a $S/F > 1$ are not necessarily model students. However, we believe they tend to present fewer behavior and academic challenges to the classroom teacher. What problems do occur tend to be transient and well within the capabilities of the average teacher to manage.

However, there are students who do not feel the same sense of belonging, acceptance, and recognition as the students described above. Frequently these students have negative interactions with parents and teachers. Many times they are excluded by their peers. More often than not, they exhibit academic difficulties. Of course these students have their good days. They sometimes have positive interactions with parents and teachers. They are occasionally selected for games by their peers, and they do display at times some academic competency. However, for these students, the total number of failures still substantially outnumber the successes, leaving the S/F ratio less than 1. Just as the occasional failure does not unduly discourage the average student, the occasional success does not encourage these students.

It is not the case that all students with a $S/F < 1$ are always disruptive or always have academic failures. However, it has been our experience that these are the students who tend to present more frequent behavior and academic challenges to the classroom teacher. The problems that do occur tend to be entrenched and may overwhelm the capabilities of the average teacher who has not restructured the way he thinks about how to manage and instruct children with behavioral problems.

Now let's look at the student with ADHD. A student who is inattentive, impulsive, and hyperactive has an increased likelihood of negative social, academic, and familial experiences. These experiences are failures. For this reason, students with ADHD tend to have a S/F ratio far lower than the average student. Therefore, students with ADHD as a group are more likely to have chronic behavior problems.

Take a moment to think of how you intervene with students who present frequent disruptive behavior. Write in the spaces below some of your interventions.

_____   _____   _____   _____

_____   _____   _____   _____

Most teachers in our workshops when asked this question volunteer interventions such as time out, being sent to the rear of the class, detentions, being sent to the principal, losing privileges like recess, public reprimands, calling parents, and assigning lower grades. All of these are similar in that they signal failure to the student. Once again she has been shown to be inadequate and has not met her need to belong, be accepted, or be recognized. These types of interventions further decrease her S/F ratio, thus increasing the likelihood of future disruptive behavior.

It is not our intention to imply that students should not experience consequences for their disruptive behavior. On the contrary, as we have stated previously, we firmly believe that all human beings need to be accountable for their behavior. However, there exist consequences discussed later in Chapters 7, 8, and 9 for inappropriate behavior that do not impact the S/F ratio in the same manner and will decrease the likelihood of future disruptive behavior.

Table 4.1 illustrates the cumulative nature of the S/F ratio involving interactions between students and their environment. It compares the hypothesized S/F ratio for average students to chronically disruptive students, including those with ADHD.

TABLE 4.1 *A Comparison of Hypothesized S/F Ratios of Average Students to Students with Chronic Disruptive Behavior, Including Those with ADHD*

	Average Students		Students With Chronic Disruptive Behavior Including Those With ADHD	
PARENTS	Mostly positive responses to daughter's or son's behavior **(success)**	Occasional negative responses to daughter's or son's behavior (failure)	Occasional positive responses to daughter's or son's behavior (success)	Mostly negative responses to daughter's or son's behavior **(failure)**
PEERS	Generally positive relationships **(success)**	Brief periods of negative interactions (failure)	Brief periods of positive interactions (success)	Generally negative relationships **(failure)**
TEACHERS	Mostly positive responses to student's behavior **(success)**	Occasional negative responses to student's behavior (failure)	Occasional positive responses to student's behavior (success)	Mostly negative responses to student's behavior **(failure)**
COMMUNITY	Frequent feelings of belonging and acceptance **(success)**	Occasional feelings of alienation and rejection (failure)	Occasional feelings of belonging and acceptance (success)	Mostly feelings of alienation and rejection **(failure)**
ACADEMIC TASKS	Frequent achievement **(success)**	Infrequent failure (failure) (success)	Infrequent achievement (success)	Frequent failure **(failure)**
NONACADEMIC TASKS	Frequent achievement **(success)**	Infrequent failure (failure)	Infrequent achievement (success)	Frequent failure **(failure)**
CUMULATIVE S/F RATIO	Success/Failure > 1		Success/Failure < 1	

MOTIVATION

The differences in the S/F ratio among students have significant impact not only on their behavior but also on the related area of their motivation. How many times have you heard comments similar to these? "I know Susan could do the work if she tried. What is it going to take to get Susan started?" Most teachers would say that Susan is not motivated.

Motivation is a measure of an individual's will to initiate and to put forth effort in activities from which some gain is sought. People may be motivated or not motivated in many different areas. For example, there is achievement motivation, learning motivation, social motivation, athletic motivation, and economic motivation. What determines whether a student is motivated or not toward school work?

Motivation has been conceptualized as equal to expectation of success multiplied by value, or $M = E \times V$ (Atkinson,1964). The variable of expectation of success is defined as an individual's belief that he or she can attain a desired goal. The variable of value is defined as the extent that this goal is important to the individual.

By examining the product of an individual's expectation and value in regard to any given endeavor, predictions can be made as to the degree of motivation that the individual brings to the task. For example, let's look at you asking someone out on a date. The expectation of success is high or low depending upon the results of previous efforts in asking other people out for dates. Value is high or low dependent upon how important it is to you that this person accepts your date offer. There are four outcomes that may result from the interaction of these variables. Table 4.2 illustrates the interaction of expectation of success and value in determining motivation, using dating as an example.

TABLE 4.2 *Motivation = Expectation of Success X Value: Asking for a Date*

| | EXPECTATION OF SUCCESS | |
	HIGH	LOW
V A L U E — HIGH	**I** M = E x V M = high x high M = (previous dating efforts were successful) x (it is important to date this person) M = HIGH	**II** M = E x V M = low x high M = (previous dating efforts were <u>unsuccessful</u>) x (it is important to date this person) M = MODERATE
— LOW	**III** M = E x V M = high x low M = (previous dating efforts were successful) x (it is <u>not</u> important to date this person) M = MODERATE	**IV** M = E x V M = low x low M = (previous dating efforts were <u>unsuccessful</u>) x (it is <u>not</u> important to date this person) M = LOW

As can be seen from Table 4.2, motivation to approach the other person and ask for a date is highest with a product of high expectation of success and high value (I). Motivation to approach the other person and ask for a date is less when one variable is high and the other is low (II, III). Motivation is lowest when both expectation of success and value are low (IV).

We assume that all students have a reasonably high expectation of success when they first start school. We also assume that all students initially place a reasonable amount of value upon doing well academically. Therefore, students begin school with a reasonably high degree of motivation.

As students progress through school, they experience both successes and failures. The average student (see Table 4.1) has far more success experiences than failures and so her S/F ratio > 1. Therefore she maintains at least a moderate expectation of success. Various activities in school may be of high, moderate or low value to this student. However, given at least a moderate expectation of success, she maintains a moderate to high level of motivation dependent upon the relative value of the activity. Her motivation generally falls in I, II, or III in Table 4.2.

What about the student who is a chronic discipline problem? She has far more failures than successes (see Table 4.1). Her S/F ratio < 1. Therefore she maintains a low expectation of success. Various activities in school may be of high, moderate, or low value to this student as well. However, given her low expectation of success, she maintains a low to, at best, moderate level of motivation depending upon the relative value of the activity. Her motivation generally falls in II, III or IV in Table 4.2.

Let's assume that two students have the same degree of value for a particular academic task. The first student has a history of substantially more successes than failures (S/F > 1) in similar academic tasks and thus has a high expectation for success. The second student has a history of substantially more failures than successes (S/F < 1) in similar academic tasks and therefore has a lower expectation of success. Because of a higher expectation of success, the first student is more motivated and puts more effort into the task. Increased effort usually leads to additional success which increases her S/F ratio even further. Therefore, the student's expectation for future success again increases resulting in additional effort which leads to more successes and a greater S/F ratio. This cycle of success (more effort, more success, more effort and so on) builds into what we term a cycle of high motivation. This cycle is illustrated in Figure 4.1. This student is unlikely to become a chronic disciplinary problem.

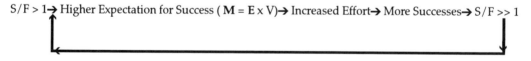

S/F > 1→ Higher Expectation for Success ($M = E \times V$)→ Increased Effort→ More Successes→ S/F >> 1

FIGURE 4.1 *The Cycle of High Motivation*

On the other hand, because of a lower expectation of success, the second student is less motivated and puts less effort into the task. Less effort usually leads to additional failures and a lowering of her S/F ratio even further. Therefore, the student's expectation for future success again decreases resulting in less effort which leads to more failure and a lower S/F ratio. This cycle of failure (less effort, more failure, less effort) we term a cycle of low motivation, illustrated in Figure 4.2. Because students with ADHD have low S/F ratios, they tend to find themselves in the cycle of low motivation. They, like other students who have S/F < 1, are at greater risk of becoming chronically disruptive.

$$S/F < 1 \rightarrow \text{Lower Expectation for Success } (M = E \times V) \rightarrow \text{Decreased Effort} \rightarrow \text{More Failure} \rightarrow S/F << 1$$

FIGURE 4.2 *The Cycle of Low Motivation*

Our formulation of motivational difficulties is applicable both to students who have more failures due to ecological factors (see Chapter 2) and, we believe, to students who have more failures due to neurological impairment such as ADHD. While the teacher cannot alter the ecology or the neurology of his students, he can alter his own behavior to increase the likelihood that the behavior of his students change. To the extent that you understand the S/F ratio and its role in motivation, you will choose behaviors which increase the likelihood that all of your students will be more successful and thus more motivated.

Intrinsic and Extrinsic Motivation

In the last section it was stated that expectation of success multiplied by value equals motivation. How do students explain success and failure and how do they determine value?

Broadly speaking students attribute their successes and failures to either causes that originate within themselves or from outside themselves (Rotter, 1966, 1975). A student who attributes her successes or failures to such factors as luck, teachers, parents, or coincidence is said to have an external locus of control. This is because her expectation of success is dependent upon factors outside her control.

A student with an internal locus of control attributes the very same successes and failures to such factors as her amount of effort, study habits, or choices she makes. This is called an internal locus of control, because her expectation of success is dependent upon factors within her control.

Generally, students attribute value to activities that provide them with opportunities to develop new competencies or that enable them to show that they are superior to others and/ or to receive rewards provided by the teacher. Students who value activities which provide them with opportunities to develop new competencies or satisfy a personal interest we term as having an internal value structure, because these outcomes are mostly independent of others. Students who value activities which provide opportunities to show their superiority to others and/or gain rewards from others are said to have an external value structure, because these outcomes are mostly dependent on others.

When a student has an internal locus of control and an internal value structure, she is intrinsically motivated, that is, the motivation comes from within herself. When a student has an external locus of control and an external value structure, she is extrinsically motivated. Her motivation comes from outside of herself. All students are either more intrinsically or extrinsically motivated depending upon the interaction of their locus of control and value structure.

A student's locus of control and value structure are greatly influenced by teacher and parent behavior. When a teacher or parent communicates to the student that success is the result of the student's effort or lack of effort, he helps the student develop an internal locus of control. When these adults communicate to students that the value of any activity is the opportunity it provides for developing new competencies, increasing maturity, and general personal growth, they are facilitating the student's internal value structure. Therefore, these parent and teacher behaviors increase the likelihood of student development of intrinsic motivation.

When a teacher or parent communicates that success is the result of luck, tricks, or due to other people's behavior, he helps the student develop an external locus of control. When these adults communicate to students that the value of any activity is the opportunity which it provides for showing superiority, gaining material rewards, or praise, they are facilitating the student's external value structure. Therefore, these parent and teacher behaviors increase the likelihood that the student will develop extrinsic motivation.

There are definite advantages in the classroom when there are students who are intrinsically motivated. Such students are less likely to be disruptive, and they show effort whether or not the teacher is monitoring them or offering any rewards. The students are less angry or frustrated with the teacher, no matter what the teacher's actions, because they attribute successes and failures to themselves and not to the teacher. In addition, when the intrinsically motivated students meet with outcomes which disappoint them, they probably will try harder.

Extrinsically motivated students tend to put forth more effort only if the teacher is monitoring them or they are gaining a specific reward. They may be angry or frustrated with the teacher, because they attribute successes and failures to teacher behavior and not to themselves. Therefore, they are more likely to be disruptive. In addition, when the extrinsically motivated students meet with outcomes which disappoint them, they likely give up, feign disinterest, or pretend to be successful. They may do this by making up excuses, saying that the work is stupid, copying homework, or lying about grades.

There are many complex factors that influence a student's propensity towards intrinsic or extrinsic motivation. We refer the interested reader to Stipek (1993) and Spaulding (1992).

SELF-ESTEEM

The S/F ratio and motivation are important components in the development of students' self-esteem. Just as teachers' self-esteem was previously conceptualized in Chapter 3, students' self-esteem may similarly be conceptualized as a sum of four factors (Coopersmith 1967): significance, competence, virtue, and power, $SE = S + C + V + P$.

Once again, significance is a person's belief that she is respected, liked, and trusted by people who are important to her. This does not mean merely that some people like her, rather that the people she wants to have like her do in fact like her. Competence is a person's sense of mastery in tasks that she values. It does not mean she is good at any old thing, but that she is good at the things which matter to her. For instance she may be a great cello player which her teachers and parents value. However, if that is not important to her, she will not feel an increased sense of competence. Virtue is a person's perceived feeling of worthiness as a result of her ability and willingness to help others. Power is a person's perception that she exerts control over important aspects of her environment. She believes that she can plan and take actions that result in predictable and desirable outcomes.

Let us assume for a moment that self-esteem is a constant. Remembering your elementary algebra, if one of the variables S,C,V, or P is reduced, another variable has to be raised correspondingly in order to maintain the constant self-esteem.

For the average student, this presents little difficulty. The average student, with a success/failure ratio > 1, has many opportunities in her life for successful experiences (review Table 4.1). If temporarily her social life is suffering (significance), she takes solace in her skills in athletics (competence). If she has a bad day on the playing field, she might be in the Scouts and doing a collection of clothing for needy children (virtue). She may know that she can go to her parents or teachers and make arrangements to change some condition or get additional help (power, significance). The average student, in short, has resources to maintain a healthy and positive feeling about herself. Teachers describe this student as having high self-esteem.

But what about the chronically disruptive student, the one with a S/F ratio < 1? Is this the student whom the other students seek out to be with? No, not usually. Is this the student most often invited for sleep overs and parties, the one who receives lots of Valentine Day cards? Again, not usually. We have found repeatedly that these students are not, in general, very popular with their peers. Thus these students' sense of *significance* will probably be low.

We know that most students who pose difficult behavioral problems struggle with academics, the very area that the majority of adults insist is the most important thing in student's lives and something that students themselves value highly, especially early in their schooling. Along with significance then, feelings of competency also suffer.

Keep in mind the summative nature of self-esteem. Therefore the remaining variables need to be very high to offset these deficits of significance and competence. The next variable is virtue. It is an unfortunate fact that students with chronic behavioral difficulties are seldom requested to help others. In addition many of them are perceived by others to be very self-absorbed. They often appear to have little knowledge or interest in the larger community whether that is the family, the classroom, or society. Virtue becomes the third variable that is reduced.

That leaves power as the last remaining variable. Unlike the average student described above, the chronically disruptive student, due to repeated negative interactions with adults, may not feel that she can go to her parents or teacher and make arrangements to change some condition or get additional help. Power, then, is also reduced.

What we now have is a student who has reduced levels of significance, competence, virtue, and power. Using the self-esteem equation, $SE = S + C + V + P$, the student has low self-esteem.

Pro-Social and Distorted Self-Esteem

Current research indicates, however, that disruptive and delinquent children sometimes have similar levels of self-esteem as the average child, as measured by standardized instruments (Kaplan 1976,1980). How can this be? Self-esteem typically is measured as a single entity, while we believe that there are at least two types of self-esteem, pro-social and distorted. Each type exists along a continuum of high to low.

For instance, we have stated that the chronically disruptive student lacks power. Many teachers say, however, that these kids have too much power. They disrupt the class, interrupt learning, perhaps even make the teacher ill. Isn't that power ? Indeed it is. This is an example of distorted power.

Self-esteem is a basic human need (Maslow,1968). If students cannot achieve self-esteem in acceptable to society or pro-social ways, they achieve self-esteem in anti-social or unacceptable to society ways. This self-esteem is called distorted self-esteem (Brendtro et al., 1990).

If we as parents and teachers do not like, respect, and trust students so that there is an increased probability that students might like, respect, and trust us, we make it more likely that they will turn to whoever gives them positive regard. A sense of significance may not be achieved only by being a class officer or everyone's favorite confidant. It may also be achieved by membership in gangs or cults, by sexual promiscuity, or by embracing the drug culture.

If students are not encouraged to value and master pro-social competencies, they are likely to value and master distorted competencies. For instance, a sense of competence may be achieved not only in the classroom or athletic field; it may also develop from being the best joint roller in the group, having the most sexual encounters in a day, knowing how to pick locks, or to steal cars.

If pro-social expressions of virtue are denied to students, they seek out opportunities to feel worthy in less desirable ways. Virtue may be achieved by volunteering at the hospital, shoveling a neighbor's walk of snow, helping another student with homework, or it may be achieved by lying to protect others, supplying buddies with drugs, or being a "lookout."

Power may be exerted by additional study to improve grades, by developing healthy eating and exercise routines to improve fitness and appearance, or it may be exercised by cheating to improve grades or by bullying and coercing classmates.

Now that you have an understanding of the importance of self-esteem, the components of self-esteem, and the pro-social and distorted ways that it may be expressed, use your knowledge to identify the components and type of self-esteem that the young man evidenced in the following anecdote.

One of the authors had the experience recently of attending juvenile court on behalf of his young client who was charged with burglary. He and another fourteen-year-old youth had broken into a neighbor's house, stolen some property, and then sold the property in order to buy drugs. The judge in the case was a well-respected but stern jurist, the kind of individual who seemed to exude Old Testament-style justice and retribution. The judge asked the author's client, "Young man, why did you do this?" The youth answered, "My friends wanted drugs, and I knew where there was an open house where we could steal stuff to sell and get money to buy drugs." The judge was not amused.

Did this boy have self-esteem? Did he demonstrate a sense of significance, virtue, and competence? The authors explain this youth's behavior as a search for self-esteem in a distorted manner through the components of virtue, significance, and competence. He wanted to help his friends; isn't this virtue? He also felt an increased sense of significance in that his friends really appreciated his efforts. His competence was clearly evident in that he knew where the house was and how to break into it. In fact the only thing that ruined the beauty of this boy's plan was that he got caught. This illustrates how the need for self-esteem may be fulfilled through distorted means.

The challenge to all responsible adults in this boy's life is how may they intervene to increase the likelihood that this young person finds virtue, significance, and competence in a pro-social way? Chapter 6 provides some of these answers.

Let's now revisit the teacher involved in a power struggle with the student, as described in the section on avoiding personalizing student behavior in Chapter 3. What is readily apparent is that the teacher experienced a deficit in positive feelings of competence, significance, and virtue. We said that the teacher in order to protect her own self-esteem moved to power. What is readily apparent is that this teacher used a distorted sense of power with the student, just as the student exhibited a distorted sense of power with the teacher. A parallel process once again is present which, in this case, impedes the possibility of movement to positive or pro-social self-esteem.

Think of how often these power struggles arise in your classroom, or indeed, in your life. How does the other person respond? If it is a true power struggle, both parties are out to win. Understanding this theory of self-esteem, it can be seen that these power struggles are nothing more than the attempt by both parties to maintain some sense of positive self-regard and to avoid the perception of failure.

These three highly interrelated and important concepts, the success/failure ratio, motivation, and self-esteem, have been merely introduced. We cannot detail all the possible combinations of the myriad interrelationships among the variables of these concepts. What we can describe are the desirable characteristics of students who are successful, motivated, and feel good about themselves in a manner which encourages positive growth and appropriate behavior.

These students

→ have a S/F ratio > 1,
→ are primarily intrinsically motivated, and
→ possess pro-social self-esteem.

Strategies to help students achieve these characteristics are discussed in Chapter 6.

SUMMARY

In this chapter, the success/failure ratio was again defined. It was shown how the interactions that students have with teachers, parents, and their peers all lead to either more failure or more success. Having a success/failure ratio either greater than 1 or less than 1 was discussed as to how this impacted upon students' future behavior. This impact was shown to be in the area of motivation.

Motivation was defined as being equal to expectation of success multiplied by value or $M = E \times V$. The magnitude of motivation is dependent on the four products of high or low expectation of success (E) multiplied by high or low value (V). The success/failure ratio directly relates to the expectation of future success and, therefore, to motivation or to the amount of effort students bring to a task. Effort towards tasks either increases the probability of success or decreases this probability, resulting in either a cycle of high motivation or a cycle of low motivation.

Internal or external loci of control and internal and external value structure were used to develop the subsuming concepts of intrinsic and extrinsic motivation. Whether a student's motivation is intrinsic or extrinsic significantly influences the student's behavior in classroom settings.

Self-esteem was described as the sum of significance, competence, virtue, and power. However, students' behavior cannot be clearly understood if self-esteem is conceptualized as a single type, either high or low. Students may express any of the components of self-esteem in acceptable to society or pro-social ways, or in unacceptable to society or distorted ways. When students are not afforded opportunities or feel incapable of expressing self-esteem in pro-social ways, as in achieving scholastically or in sports or by being involved in their community or family, they are likely to express self-esteem in a distorted manner that is, for example, by joining gangs, being promiscuous, or being disruptive in the classroom.

Finally, it was concluded that students who are likely to behave appropriately and achieve academically are those having a S/F ratio > 1, who are intrinsically motivated, and possess pro-social self-esteem.

Concept Map

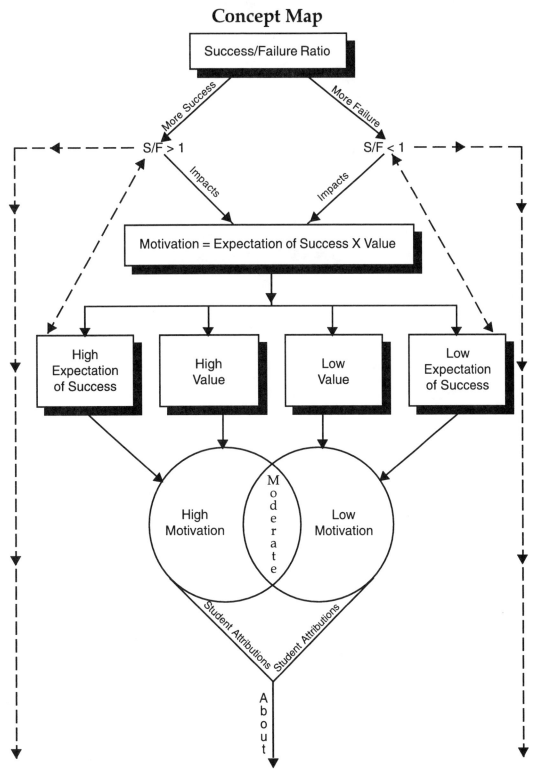

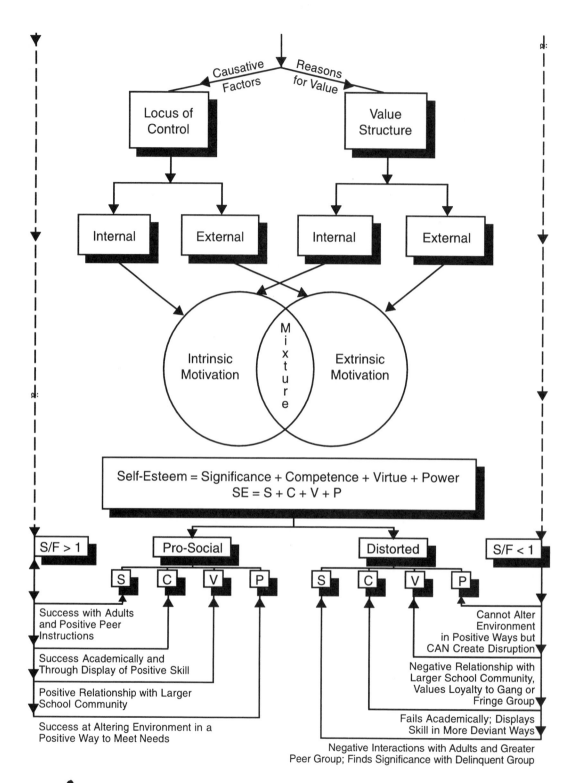

REFERENCES

Adler, A.(1963).The Problem Child, v, New York: Capricorn.

Atkinson, J. (1964). *An Introduction to Motivation*, Princeton, NJ: Van Nostrand.

Brendtro, L. K., Brockenleg, M., & VanBocken, S. (1990). *Reclaiming Youth at Risk, Our Hope for the Future*. Bloomington, IN: National Education Service.

Coopersmith, S. (1967). *The Antecedents of Self Esteem*. San Francisco, CA: W.H. Freedman.

Gever, B. (1991). Psychiatric Manifestations of Learning Disorders. Reading, Writing, and Learning Disorders 7, 231–242.

Gever, B. (1982). Classroom Management Workshop, Emporium, PA.

James, W. (1890). *Principles of Psychology* (2 vols.). New York: H. Holt and Company.

Kaplan, H.B. (1976). Self-attitudes and deviant response. Social Forces, 54, 788-801.

Kaplan, H.B.(1980). *Deviant Behavior in Defense of Self*. New York: Academic Press.

Maslow, A. (1968). *Toward a Psychology of Being*. New York: D. Van Nostrand.

Rotter, J. (1975). Some problems and misconceptions related to the construct of internal versus external control of reinforcement. *Journal of Consulting and Clinical Psychology, 43*, 56-67.

Rotter, J. (1966). Generalized expectations for internal versus external control of reinforcement. *Psychological Monographs, 1*, 609.

Spaulding, C. (1992). *Motivation in the Clasroom*, New York: McGraw-Hill, Inc.

Stipek, D. J. (1993). *Motivation to Learn, From Theory to Practice*, 2nd ed. Boston: Allyn and Bacon.

FREQUENTLY ASKED QUESTIONS

1. It was stated that many traditional management interventions are perceived as failures by students and they serve to lower the students' success/failure ratio. However, many students perceive being asked to leave the room or being sent to the principal's office as being successes. Doesn't this then raise the success/failure ratio?

2. What about the student who comes to class, sits in the back of the room, interacts with no one, does no work, and is not disruptive? Does this student have distorted or pro-social self-esteem?

3. Since our culture is so extrinsically motivated, am I not doing my students a disservice by trying to increase their intrinsic motivation?

4. You said previously that cognitive and moral development naturally lead to more disruptive behaviors. Does this mean that distorted self-esteem is normal too?

5. Do students with distorted self-esteem really feel good about themselves or are they just pretending to feel good about themselves?

6. I have students in my class whose ability makes it very unlikely that they can achieve success, no matter how much effort they put into an academic task. How can these students ever develop an internal locus of control?

Chapter 5

Teacher Authority and Its Use

INTRODUCTION

E very school consists of teachers with different philosophies about the use of authority in classroom management. These different philosophies are reflected in the variety of strategies used to manage student behavior. It may seem that the strategy chosen by the teacher is less important than the desired outcome, which is a classroom relatively free of disruptive behavior. What this point of view fails to take into consideration is the effect of the various strategies upon future student behavior, such as when the teacher leaves the room, or is absent, and on student behavior in other classes. The effect of any strategy upon future student behavior is dependent upon how that strategy impacts the student's success/failure ratio, motivation, and self-esteem.

In this chapter we explore the derivation of authority and its classification into four broad categories. The authority base that you use depends upon your beliefs about the role of teachers and the role of students in managing student behavior. The importance of understanding the differences among these authority bases is that the beliefs that a teacher holds about the nature and use of authority in the classroom influences what behavior teachers choose when attempting to manage student behavior. These teacher behaviors have a significant impact upon students' success/failure ratio, motivation, and self-esteem. In addition, they strongly influence the teacher's stress level. Therefore, the way that teachers use authority has a significant influence on the probability of the recurrence of appropriate or inappropriate student behavior.

THE NATURE OF AUTHORITY

In your life, whom do you consider an authority? By this we mean whom do you voluntarily go to for advice, or whose advice might you seriously consider prior to making a decision? List each of these people in Table 5.1. Next ask yourself why you listen to these people? We have asked many teachers these same questions. Table 5.1 lists a few of their responses to help you get started. Fill in as many others as you can.

TABLE 5.1 *Authorities in Our Lives*

PERSON IN AUTHORITY	REASON THESE PEOPLE HAVE AUTHORITY
1. parents	they care, trust, and respect me
2. police officer	they have formal responsibilities backed by the legal system
3. auto mechanic	they have a specialized body of knowledge
4. boss	they can write me a positive or negative evaluation
5.	
6.	
7.	
8.	
9.	
10.	
11.	
12.	
13.	
14.	
15.	

Authority figures typically fall into four categories. We have placed the first entry into each category in Table 5.2 to reflect how many teachers in our workshops have categorized these authority figures. Parents are placed into Category 1. Teachers tell us that they view their parents as authority figures, because their parents communicate to them that they love, trust, and respect them and therefore have their best interests in mind. Using your entries in Table 5.1, identify individuals whom you invest with authority for the same reason that you invest your parents with authority. Place them in Category 1.

Auto mechanics are placed in category 2. They have authority because people need their specialized body of knowledge of how to fix cars. Identify those on your list whom you invest with authority because of your need for their specialized knowledge. Add them to Category 2.

Police officers are placed into category 3. Their authority results from formal governmental responsibilities to uphold the law which is supported by our society. Are there any people on your list with societal supported responsibilities? If so, write them in Category 3.

People on your list who have the capability to reward and punish you and do so, such as a boss, are placed in Category 4.

TABLE 5.2 *Categories of Authority*

CATEGORY 1	CATEGORY 2	CATEGORY 3	CATEGORY 4
parents	auto mechanic	police officer	boss

French and Raven (1960), studied how people are invested with authority. They identified four authority bases: referent, expert, legitimate, and coercive, sometimes called reward/punishment.

People who demonstrate to us that they trust, respect, and care about us are said to be invested with referent authority. Such people often are parents, spouses, best friends, siblings, and personal mentors. A person does not have to have a title or degree to be perceived as possessing referent authority. These individuals are respected, and their advice is sought or seriously considered because of their positive regard for us and their concern about us. Make certain that Category 1 includes only those people whom you consider to possess referent authority.

The people who have expert authority are those whose advice we seriously consider or follow because they possess specialized bodies of knowledge or experience that we do not have ourselves and we need. Examples of those with expert authority are auto mechanics, lawyers, doctors, plumbers, and psychologists. These people obtain their expertise usually through long years of schooling or on the job training. What's important is that their authority comes from the knowledge that they possess and not necessarily from their regard for us. Expert authority is Category 2.

People to whom we pay serious attention solely because their formal responsibilities and actions are sanctioned by our society are termed as having legitimate authority. Examples of people with legitimate authority are lifeguards, traffic directors at highway construction sites, police officers, judges, and internal revenue service agents. We perceive them as authority figures because they carry out duties that are legally assigned them by local, state, or federal governmental agencies. There are often legal consequences for not heeding the advice of individuals with legitimate authority when they are performing their prescribed duties.

Coercive authority is reserved for people who have the power and use it to reward or punish you. A person at the coercive level is not likely to be viewed as deriving authority from any other base. Examples of people with coercive power include a boss or supervisor who could fire or demote you, or promote you and give you a raise, or just a plain bully. Table 5.3 summarizes our analyses of authority bases thus far.

TABLE 5.3 *Summary of Authority Bases*

POWER BASES	REFERENT	EXPERT	LEGITIMATE	COERCIVE
ATTRIBUTES	cares, trusts, respects you	has specialized body of knowledge	is sanctioned by society	gives rewards and punishment
MEMBERSHIP	parents spouses best friends	doctors plumbers attorneys	life guards police officers judges	bosses bullies

If teachers are on your list, into which category did you place them? In our workshops, participants place teachers in every category. The category teachers are placed in depends upon what specific teacher a participant has in mind.

In Chapter 4, we asked you to think about the best and the worst teachers you ever had. At this time recall who these teachers were. Ask yourself into which category does your best teacher belong and into which category does your worst teacher belong? While most teachers operate from more than one authority base, it usually is possible to identify one predominant base. To help you categorize these two teachers, ask yourself the following questions: Why did you behave appropriately for your best teacher? Was it because the teacher cared, trusted, and respected you? If you answered "yes," then your teacher had referent authority. Was it because the teacher really knew the subject, made it interesting, and made certain that you understood it? If you answered "yes," then your teacher had expert authority. Was it because the teacher told you that you had to behave appropriately, because "they said so" or because "they were the teacher?" If so, then the teacher had legitimate authority. Was it because the teacher was quick to reward you when you behaved and quick to punish you when you did not behave? If so, the teacher had coercive authority. Next, ask yourself the same questions about your worst teacher to determine which authority base this teacher used.

We have conducted this activity with thousands of teachers. Almost without exception, the best teachers are perceived to be referent or expert authorities, while the worst teachers are viewed as legitimate or coercive authorities.

If your students were asked these same questions, into which authority base would they place you? Some teachers who have asked their students to answer these questions are surprised to discover that their students think that they operate from the same authority base as the teacher's own worst teacher. The reason teachers are often surprised by student perceptions is that teachers' actual use of authority is not always congruent with their beliefs.

RELATED MODELS OF CLASSROOM MANAGEMENT

Wolfgang and Glickman (1980) analyzed the various ways that teachers manage students and grouped them into three models of classroom management: noninterventionist, interactionist, and interventionist. Interestingly, as discussed in the later section on characteristics of teacher authority bases, each authority base that we are studying is related to one or more of these management models.

Noninterventionist

From the name of this approach you may think that a noninterventionist teacher would be a hands off, anything goes type of person. However, nothing is further from the truth. Noninterventionists are highly-skilled, well-trained professionals who have an explicitly defined philosophy about the role of the teacher and the student in the educational process. Noninterventionist teachers believe that students are capable of, want to, and will control themselves, if given opportunities to do so.

The noninterventionist school of thought includes models of classroom management that are the most student-centered. However, these teachers are realistic and realize that in real classrooms, discipline problems arise. To manage these problems, the noninterventionist teacher focuses on student self-management strategies such as individual problem-solving, peer mediation, classroom meetings, and other cooperative conflict resolution strategies. These strategies, by encouraging students to express their feelings in an appropriate manner, decrease the likelihood of disruptive acting out.

Pragmatically, self-control is a long term goal, especially since most students are rarely given the opportunities or taught all the skills to develop and demonstrate self-control in traditional classrooms. As a result, many students expect teachers to jump in and take control. However when teachers do jump in, students are denied opportunities to learn one of the most important lifelong skills, controlling one's own behavior.

Interactionist

Interactionists believe that appropriate student behavior is a shared responsibility between the teacher and her students. Many teachers find that this school of thought best reflects their beliefs and the reality of what actually happens in their classrooms. These teachers desire students to assume self-control but understand that for many reasons, some are unable or unwilling to do so. Student input into the development of classroom rules, student choice about what and how they learn, and responsibility for self-control are important. However, the interactionist teacher reserves for herself final say for any classroom decision. She is inclined to veto student decisions that she believes may lead to negative consequences rather than letting students fully experience the results of their own choices. When a discipline problem is observed, interactionists intervene more quickly than the noninterventionist.

The first interventions are subtle and nonverbal, intended to provide the student with the opportunity to manage herself. If unsuccessful, the teacher next is likely to intervene with verbal requests and demands, which are then quickly followed by consequences if the student does not comply.

Interactionists recognize the importance of effective teaching for both prevention of discipline problems and student academic growth. However, they tend to use more teacher directed strategies than noninterventionists who use more student-centered strategies.

As an interactionist, a teacher must be cautious not to forget that with practice and appropriate teacher expectations, most students can learn and accept more responsibility for self-control. Difficulty arises when teachers take on more and more of the total responsibility while giving students less and less responsibility, which actually decreases the likelihood that students will learn self-control.

Interventionist

Interventionists are just about at the opposite end of the continuum from noninterventionists in their belief that classroom management must be primarily under the control of the teacher. They believe that teachers have the formal and legal responsibility to control student behavior in the classroom. Interventionists also believe that students are more likely to behave appropriately when the teacher rapidly and predictably intervenes at the first sign of inappropriate behavior. Because of the time it takes for students to develop self control, interventionist teachers believe that they save valuable time by getting right to the point and acting immediately to stop the unwanted behavior. A look followed by a verbal demand for appropriate behavior is quickly followed by consequences if there is not student compliance.

Interventionists shape student behavior by controlling the positive and negative consequences of behavior. Positive behavior is quickly reinforced with rewards while negative behavior is punished. The rewards and punishments are sometimes operationalized into formal delivery systems of behavioral contracts, token economies, and other contingency based management systems. Many times group rewards and punishments are contingent upon each student's compliance or noncompliance with the teacher-designed classroom rules. Figure 5.1 illustrates where each management model is placed along a continuum of student control of student behavior to teacher control of student behavior.

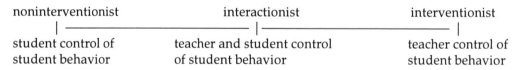

Figure 5.1 *Continuum of Control of Student Behavior*

CHARACTERISTICS OF TEACHER AUTHORITY BASES

In reality, teachers use strategies from all four bases, depending upon the specific classroom situation. Nevertheless, teachers use more strategies from one predominant authority base and so may be classified as having this base. For the purpose of clarity, we describe the characteristics of each authority base as if it were a discrete category and identify which model(s) of classroom management, noninterventionist, interactionist, or interventionist is most congruent.

Your understanding of the following material is dependent upon a thorough understanding of the concepts of the success/failure ratio, motivation, and self-esteem. Take a moment to review these concepts explained in Chapter 4.

Referent Authority

A teacher with referent authority believes that students have the ability and responsibility to behave appropriately in the classroom. She believes that students will use their ability and accept responsibility for self-control when they are in environments in which the teacher shows sincere interest in students and shows respect for students' competence and opinions.

A teacher utilizing referent authority will likely display the following behaviors in order to prevent discipline problems. She demonstrates that she is sincerely interested in the individual student as a unique and valuable person, shows respect for student opinions, and trusts the student to make appropriate choices. Differences among students are recognized and respected in all student/teacher interactions. To intervene when disruptive behavior occurs, she likely uses techniques which do not embarrass or draw undue attention to the student. She speaks to the student privately, uses empathy to understand the student's frame of mind, and encourages the student to problem-solve in order to reassert self-control.

The Impact of Referent Authority on the Success/Failure Ratio, Motivation, and Self-Esteem

Teachers using referent authority increase the success of student/teacher interactions by ensuring that these interactions are positive. They encourage the development of an internal locus of control by stressing that students have the responsibility for their own behavior and that students play a major role in the development of class rules and guidelines. In addition, because the teacher stresses that all people are to be respected and treated fairly, the value structure of students is more likely to be internal. The motivation for appropriate behavior is therefore intrinsic.

Teachers using referent authority foster pro-social self-esteem by increasing students' sense of significance. In addition, pro-social power and competence are increased by affirming student responsibility for self-control and by giving students significant control over the classroom environment. By communicating each student's value to the class community as a whole, students' virtue is increased. The teacher minimizes the probability that students will need to find their self-esteem through distorted means.

Use of this authority base tends to be effective for students of all ages because individual differences are considered. Thus, the basic need of all human beings to be appreciated and respected by others is met (Maslow, 1968).

Most teachers using referent authority use primarily noninterventionist management models. The better known models of management that are grounded in the noninterventionist philosophy include those espoused by Gordon (1974), Ginott (1972), Berne (1964), and Harris, (1969).

Expert Authority

In the expert authority base, the teacher believes that students have the ability and responsibility to behave appropriately in the classroom. Further, she believes that students use their ability and accept responsibility for self-control when they are in classrooms in which the teacher designs effective learning environments. Such a learning environment is created when 1) student interest is captured and maintained, 2) material is clearly presented to enhance student understanding, and 3) many opportunities are provided for students to demonstrate their understanding.

A teacher utilizing expert authority prevents discipline problems by using instructional techniques and planning instructional activities, which increase the likelihood of student success and by making on-task behavior more interesting than disruptive behavior. Differences among students are considered and respected because this is inherent in effective instruction. In intervening when disruptive behavior occurs, a teacher operating from the expert base may use any effective management technique; however, due to her emphasis on effective instruction, she most likely uses techniques which redirect student interest to the lesson.

The Impact of Expert Authority on the Success/Failure Ratio, Motivation, and Self-Esteem

Because the student in a classroom of a teacher using expert authority learns that she can be successful, she experiences an increase in her internal locus of control. By designing lessons that students find relevant, teachers increase the likelihood that students have an internal value structure. The motivation for positive behavior is therefore intrinsic.

Teachers using expert authority impact student pro-social self-esteem by increasing the students' sense of academic competence. With the application of this newly found competence comes an increase in power. Thus, like the teacher using referent authority, the teacher using expert authority minimizes the probability that students need to find their self-esteem through distorted means.

The use of expert authority is effective for students of all ages because effective instruction focuses upon student interest, understanding, and success. It is even more effective for the older student whose interest may be more difficult to capture and who is required to learn more complex material. Therefore, a less skilled teacher will have even more difficulty with this population.

Most expert teachers align themselves with the noninterventionist and/or interactionist management models. The best known models of classroom management that employ the interactionist approach were developed by Dreikurs and Bassel (1971) and Glasser (1969).

Legitimate Authority

In the legitimate authority base, just like in the referent and expert bases, the teacher believes that students have the ability and responsibility to behave appropriately in the classroom. However, she believes students use their ability and accept responsibility for self-control when they are in environments in which they clearly understand the legal authority of the teacher and that the teacher is in charge.

A teacher utilizing legitimate authority may display the following behaviors intended to prevent discipline problems. She clearly communicates to the students what her role as teacher is and what their role is as students. Unlike teachers using referent and expert authority, teachers using legitimate authority are less likely to take individual student differences into account when formulating expectations for student behavior, because individual differences are not mitigating circumstances when it comes to what is and what is not appropriate classroom behavior. When disruptive behavior occurs, she likely uses techniques that remind the student that she, the teacher, is in charge and shows what exact behavior is required in the classroom. The message this teacher is most likely to send to a student is, "It's my way or the highway."

The Impact of Legitimate Authority on the Success/Failure Ratio, Motivation, and Self-Esteem

Because there is little, if any, ambiguity as to who is in charge of the classroom and what is expected of the student, students with a need for a high degree of structure may be successful in these classrooms. On the other hand, students needing a high degree of autonomy or less structure may strongly resist these teachers, resulting in negative interactions between the teacher and students or an increase in failure experiences. Student success or failure is therefore uncertain and very dependent upon each individual student's needs.

Teachers using legitimate authority encourage the development of an external locus of control by reminding students that it is the teacher, and only the teacher, who determines appropriate student behavior. If students behave appropriately, it is because they value the legal authority of the teacher. Because the nature of legal authority is externally determined, the effect upon student value structure tends to be external. Teachers who mainly rely on legitimate authority foster extrinsic motivation.

Students in the classroom of a teacher using legitimate authority are inclined to feel a lack of power since many of the opportunities for student control are taken over by the teacher. Since power is lessened for students, their pro-social self-esteem is therefore dependent upon increases in opportunities for significance, competence, and virtue. To the extent that these three variables are not increased, the student becomes more likely to express her self-esteem in a distorted manner.

This authority base tends to be more effective for students at the elementary level and loses effectiveness as students become more cognitively and morally sophisticated. The rationale, "You'll do it because I'm the teacher," is no longer adequate for older students, who naturally question authority at this time in their lives. Most teachers using legitimate authority align themselves with the interactionist or interventionist management models.

Coercive Authority

In the coercive authority base, as in the three other authority bases, the teacher believes that students have the ability and responsibility to behave appropriately in the classroom. In addition, she believes that students use their ability and accept responsibility for self-control, primarily when they are in environments in which the teacher uses positive reinforcement and punishment to influence student behavior.

A teacher utilizing coercive authority may attempt to prevent disruptive behavior by designing a system of rewards and incentives for appropriate behavior and a system of increasingly unpleasant consequences for inappropriate behavior. Like teachers using legitimate authority, teachers using coercive authority are less likely to take individual student differences into account when attempting to understand student behavior. When disruptive behavior occurs she may communicate to the student that a negative consequence is imminent if the behavior continues. If the student does not comply in a timely manner, the teacher administers the consequence.

The Impact of Coercive Authority on the Success/Failure Ratio, Motivation, and Self-Esteem

The primary focus of teachers using this authority base is on appropriate behavior. If students behave appropriately, they have successful experiences. If they behave inappropriately, they have failure experiences. Because the teacher has absolute control of all rewards and punishments, students are encouraged toward an external locus of control. To the extent that the student either desires the reward or fears the negative consequences, her value structure is external. Teachers using coercive authority clearly encourage extrinsic motivation in their students.

Because the contingencies of rewards and punishments are at the sole discretion of the teacher, students often feel manipulated and so experience a reduction in their sense of power. In addition, because only certain behavior is rewarded, fewer students feel competent. Therefore, unless significant opportunities exist for students to display pro-social virtue or to feel significant, students likely resort to developing self-esteem in distorted ways.

This authority base tends to be more effective at the primary grade level but rapidly loses effectiveness as students get older, until it is relatively ineffective at the upper secondary grade level. This is due, in part, because older students are at higher levels of moral development, where their decisions are based upon considerations other than extrinsic contingencies and due also to the difficulty of finding meaningful rewards and punishments as children get older. There are many additional problems associated with the use of rewards and punishments that are discussed in Chapter 6.

Teachers who use coercive authority, for the most part, align themselves with interventionist classroom management models. The best known interventionist models are those developed by Axelrod (1977), Canter (1978), Dobson (1970), and Valentine (1987).

As stated previously, the pragmatic teacher moves among authority bases, because she realizes that one authority base is not effective with all children in all situations. However, each teacher has an affinity for one particular authority base because that base is most congruent with her beliefs about the role of teachers and students. Study Table 5.3 to determine which authority base you most often use or want to use. You now know more about the nature of authority in general and know specifically the effect of the use of different authority bases upon students' success/failure ratio, motivation, and self-esteem. Are you comfortable that the manner in which you express authority is congruent with your beliefs and with the desired outcome you want for your students? If not, remember if you continue to do what you've done, you'll continue to get what you got. Therefore, it may be time to consider a change in your behavior.

TABLE 5.3 *Comparison of Authority Bases' Characteristics*

AUTH. BASES	REFERENT	EXPERT	LEGITIMATE	COERCIVE
ATTRIBUTES	cares, trusts, respects	has specialized body of knowledge	is sanctioned by society	gives rewards and punishment
MEMBERSHIP	parents, spouses, best friends	doctors, plumbers, attorneys	lifeguards, police officers, judges	punitive supervisors, bullies
TEACHER BEHAVIORS INTENDED TO PREVENT DISCIPLINE PROBLEMS	takes a sincere interest in the individual student, respects student opinions, trusts the student to make appropriate choices	uses instructional techniques and plans instructional activities which make on-task behavior more interesting than disruptive behavior	communicates to the student what is the role of the teacher and what is the role of the student	designs and uses a system of rewards and incentives for appropriate behavior and punishment for inappropriate behavior
IMPORTANCE OF INDIVIDUAL STUDENT DIFFERENCES	differences among students are considered and respected	differences among students are considered and respected	differences among students are less likely to be considered and respected	differences among students are less likely to be considered and respected
TEACHER BEHAVIORS USED TO MANAGE DISCIPLINE PROBLEMS	uses techniques which do not embarrass or draw undue attention to the student, speaks to the student privately, and uses empathy to understand the student's frame of mind, encourages the student to problem-solve in order to reassert self-control	uses any management technique, however, due to her focus on effective instruction most likely uses techniques which redirect student interest to the lesson	uses techniques that remind the student who is in charge and what the appropriate behavior of the student must be in the classroom	uses behaviors that signal the student that punishment is forthcoming. If the behavior continues, administers the punishment

AUTH. BASES	REFERENT	EXPERT	LEGITIMATE	COERCIVE
SUCCESS/ FAILURE RATIO	increases success	increases success	uncertain, dependent upon individual student's need for structure	uncertain, dependent upon individual student's behavior
TYPE OF STUDENT MOTIVATION	intrinsic	intrinsic	extrinsic	extrinsic
SELF-ESTEEM	increases pro-social significance, competence and power	increases pro-social competence and power	decreases pro-social power	decreases pro-social power and competence
FACILITATES STUDENT SELF-CONTROL	yes	yes	no	no
NEED FOR TEACHER CONTROL OF STUDENT BEHAVIOR	low, due to increase in student self-control	low, due to increase in student self-control	high, due to decrease in student self-control	high, due to decrease in student self-control
POTENTIAL FOR STUDENT/ TEACHER CONFRON-TATION	low, due to increase in student self-control	low, due to increase in student self-control	moderate, due to decrease in student self-control	high, due to decrease in student self-control
POTENTIAL FOR TEACHER STRESS	low, due to lowered potential for student/teacher confrontation	low, due to lowered potential for student/teacher confrontation	moderate, due to moderate potential for student/teacher confrontation	high, due to increase in potential for student/teacher confrontation
AGE EFFECTIVE-NESS	all ages	all ages	more effective at elementary level, loses effectiveness as student gets older	more effective at primary level, rapidly loses effectiveness as student gets older, relatively ineffective at secondary level

AUTH. BASES	REFERENT	EXPERT	LEGITIMATE	COERCIVE
MANAGEMENT MODEL	non-interventionist	non-interventionist, interactionist	interactionist, interventionist	interventionist
THEORIST	Berne, Ginott, Gordon, Harris	Berne, Ginott, Gordon, Harris Driekurs, Glasser	Driekurs, Glasser Axelrod, Cantor, Dobson, Valentine	Axelrod, Cantor, Dobson, Valentine
CAUTIONS	do not confuse liking, caring about, and respecting a child with using that child to fulfill your own personal needs for significance, caring, and respect	requires a great deal of dedication and effort to remain at the forefront of your profession	changes in society have lessened the effectiveness of this type of authority	there are many problems with using authority based in coercion

YOUR CHOICE OF AUTHORITY BASE AND MANAGEMENT MODELS

If you agree with the authors and want to facilitate student development so they have a success/failure ratio > 1, are intrinsically motivated, and have high pro-social self-esteem, you are likely to conclude, based upon this chapter, that the referent and expert authority bases are preferable. If so, you will concentrate on primarily using them. Also, you will want to use techniques from the noninterventionist or interactionist management models.

At this point, consider how your behavior may change if you have a class with some highly disruptive students including several with ADHD? How can a teacher remain non-interventionist? The answer is, you can't. Not if you care about getting through a curriculum and ensuring that the other students in your classroom have an opportunity to learn. Chronically disruptive students push you in the direction of intervention. If you are a noninterventionist with these students, you are not effective and you increase the likelihood that chaos will reign in your classroom.

So you need to be an interventionist, at least some of the time. However, we stated that an interventionist approach decreases student success, encourages extrinsic motivation, and affords fewer opportunities for pro-social self-esteem. The question for you then becomes, "How can I intervene in a manner that preserves a success/failure ratio > 1, intrinsic motivation, and pro-social self-esteem?" Let's examine how this can be accomplished.

Students have choices. If a student chooses to fail, meaning that they insist upon inappropriate behavior even after having this behavior brought to their attention, it negatively impacts the success/failure ratio. Therefore, you cannot turn this into a success. You can, however, preserve intrinsic motivation by encouraging an internal locus of control through choosing interventions that 1) respect students' right to choose, 2) communicate student responsibility to choose, 3) allow time for students to make these choices, and 4) provide for explicit student understanding of the outcomes of their choices. If the student chooses to continue her disruptive behavior, predictable and consistent consequences that are logically related to the disruptive behavior are provided. To the extent that the student believes that the teacher values her as an individual, even when the student makes poor choices, and respects the student's autonomy and power to choose, the teacher protects and even helps to increase the student's pro-social self-esteem through significance and power.

So why not be an interventionist all the time? Because noninterventionist techniques increase the probability that all students will exercise appropriate self-control. Therefore the need for teacher intervention is reduced, while interventionist techniques, because they focus on teacher control of student behavior, increase the likelihood of the need for teacher intervention in the future. Brendtro, et al. (1990), warns that teacher control becomes self-perpetuating, in that the more a teacher controls students, the more likely it is that they will need to continue to control students.

SUMMARY

This chapter described four authority bases that teachers use to manage student behavior: referent, expert, legitimate, and coercive. Teachers perceived as using referent authority are those who use primarily affective means to impact student behavior. They communicate to students a sincere liking, trust, and respect. Teachers perceived as exercising expert authority use primarily professional methodology to impact student behavior. They design and deliver meaningful lessons using effective pedagogy that increases the likelihood that students will succeed. Teachers using legitimate authority influence student behavior by relying upon their legal status as teachers. They clearly communicate that they have been given and accept the responsibility for being in charge of the classroom including the design and enforcement of classroom rules. Teachers with coercive authority rely upon contingency-based management to influence student behavior. These teachers reward students for appropriate behavior and deliver negative consequences for disruptive behavior.

In practice, teachers move among bases, because they understand that one base is not appropriate for all students in all situations. However, teachers do have a primary affinity for a specific authority base dependent upon their individual beliefs about the teacher role and student role in managing student behavior.

To assist teachers in understanding each authority base and to help them determine the one toward which they have the greatest affinity, each base was analyzed over a number of dimensions. These dimensions are: 1) teacher behaviors intended to prevent discipline problems, 2) teacher behaviors used to intervene when managing disruptive behavior, 3) importance of individual differences, 4) facilitation of student self-control, 5) potential for student/teacher conflict, 6) need for teacher control of student behavior, 7) potential for teacher stress, and 8) age effectiveness.

Three management models were also described, noninterventionists, interactionist, and interventionist. Each model was identified with the authority base that has the best philosophical fit. Particular importance was given to how each authority base impacts students' success/failure ratio, intrinsic motivation, and pro-social self-esteem. It was concluded that the referent and expert authority bases were those most likely to facilitate students' success/failure ratio > 1, intrinsic motivation, and pro-social self-esteem.

Finally, the paradox of the likely need to be an interventionist with chronically disruptive students while still attempting to facilitate students' success/failure > 1, intrinsic motivation, and pro-social self-esteem was presented.

Concept Map

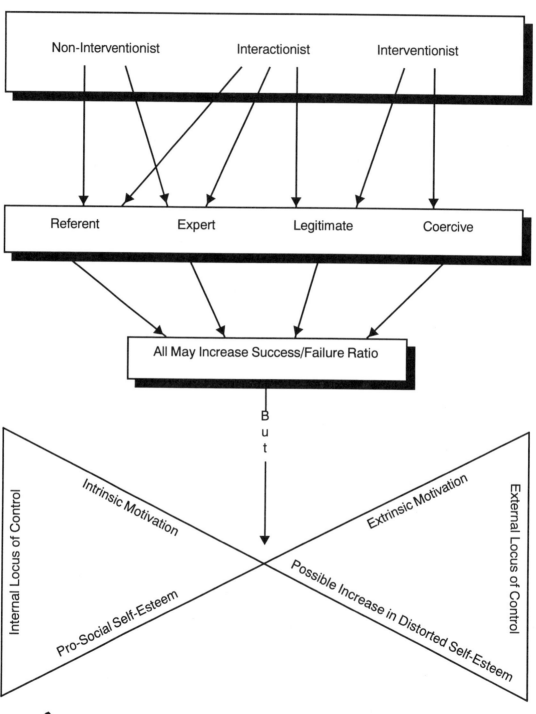

REFERENCES

Axelrod, S. (1977). *Behavior Modification for the Classroom Teacher*. New York, NY: McGraw-Hill.

Berne, E. (1964). *Games People Play: The Psychology of Human Relations*. New York, NY: Grove Press.

Brendtro, L. K., Brokenleg, M., and Van Bockern, S. (1990). *Reclaiming Youth at Risk: Our Hope for the Future*. Bloomington, IN: National Education Service.

Canter, L. (1978). *Assertive Discipline*. New York, NY: Wadsworth.

Dobson, J. (1970). *Dare to Discipline*. Wheaton, IL: Tyndale House.

Dreikurs, R. and Bassel, P. (1971). *Discipline Without Tears*. New York, NY: Hawthorne.

French, J. R. P., and Raven, B. (1960). In D. Cartwright and A. Zander (Eds.), I. Evaston, IL: Row-Peterson.

Ginott, H. (1972). *Between Teacher and Child*. New York, NY: Peter H. Wyden.

Glasser, W. (1969). *Schools Without Failure*. New York, NY: Harper and Row.

Gordon, T. (1964). *Teacher Effectiveness Training*. Peter H. Wyden.

Harris, T. (1969). I'm O.K.; You're O.K.: *A Practical Guide to Transactional Analysis*. New York, NY: Harper and Row.

Maslow, A (1968). *Toward a Psychology of Being*. New York: D. Van Nostrand.

Wolfgang, C. and Glickman, C. (1980). *Solving Discipline Problems: Strategies for Classroom Teachers*. Boston, MA: Allyn and Bacon.

Valentine, M. R. (1987). *How to Deal With Discipline Problems in the Schools: A Practical Guide for Educators*. Dubuque, IA: Kendall/Hunt.

FREQUENTLY ASKED QUESTIONS

1. If students with ADHD are relatively insensitive to rewards and punishment, then why does coercive authority seem to work for them?

2. Is it possible for a new teacher to have referent authority, or does it take a long time to develop?

3. How can I use different techniques of classroom management with different kids without the students feeling as though they are being treated unfairly?

4. If a classroom is non-interventionist with the teacher allowing the students to work out their own problems, won't the class be out of control at some point?

5. Being a new teacher, how will I know what methods and power bases to choose?

6. Doesn't strong discipline like that of the coercive base build moral character?

7. Aren't there some students who understand that teachers really mean business only when the threat of punishment is present?

Chapter 6

Prevention of Discipline Problems: Effective Instruction, Motivation, Self-Esteem

INTRODUCTION

We have stressed our belief throughout this book that the only behavior teachers can control is their own. In addition, we have explained our further belief that students who have a success/failure ratio > 1, intrinsic motivation, and pro-social self-esteem are less likely to exhibit disruptive behavior. Relating these two ideas, the question arises as to what teacher behaviors in the classroom are likely to have a positive impact on students' success/failure ratios, intrinsic motivation, and pro-social self-esteem? Brophy provides an answer to this question: "Research findings converge on the conclusion that teachers who approach classroom management as a process of establishing and maintaining effective learning environments tend to be more successful than teachers who place more emphasis on their roles as authority figures or disciplinarians" (1988a, p.1). We think that "effective learning environments" prevent disruptive behavior, and effective learning environments are created when teachers use effective instructional techniques and behaviors designed to increase student motivation and self-esteem. This chapter details examples of teacher behaviors that facilitate students' success/failure ratios >1, intrinsic motivation, and pro-social self-esteem.

In the very first chapter we stated that there is nothing vastly different that you need to do in instruction and management of disruptive students, including those with ADHD, than of other students; you just have to do it better. This chapter explains how you begin to do it better.

EFFECTIVE INSTRUCTION

Although it is beyond the scope of this book to provide an exhaustive review of effective instruction, this chapter serves as an introduction to effective instruction. A common concern of many educators is how to be sure that one is using effective instruction. Fortunately, the teaching profession has a rich body of research that delineates best professional practices. Therefore, our teaching behaviors may be compared and contrasted to these findings of past, present, and on-going research to provide us with insight into the degree to which we are employing effective instructional practices.

As in any profession, our best professional practices are not static, but instead dynamically change, as researchers formulate and study new approaches and strategies. Due to recent reconceptualizations of the teaching/learning process, the practice of teaching is presently undergoing renewed scrutiny.

Historically, educational researchers focused on identifying and describing those teacher behaviors significantly related to improved student academic achievement. Achievement was typically defined as lower-level cognitive skills, such as recall and comprehension, taught by direct teacher instruction and measured by the traditional paper and pencil objective test (Brophy, 1988b). This avenue of research came under attack in the mid 1980's, primarily because of its focus on low-level cognitive processing skills. Spurred on by discoveries in cognitive psychology focusing on the active construction of knowledge by the learner (Piaget and Inhelder, 1971, Sigel and Cocking, 1977, Copple, et al, 1984, von Glasersfeld, 1981, Jackson, 1986, Gardner, 1991) and historical philosophical perceptions as to the role of the learner (Dewey, 1938), educational researchers began to focus on how students learn higher-level cognitive skills rather than on how teachers teach lower-level cognitive skills. Of course teachers still play a pivotal role in the teaching/learning process. However, the emphasis has shifted away from teachers disseminating knowledge didactically, seeking correct simplistic answers to validate learning, and separating assessment of learning from the actual process of learning. The emphasis now has moved toward teachers providing opportunities for students to interactively construct knowledge, seeking students' extended explanations to assess their understanding, and integrating assessment with learning through students' portfolios that contain products of their work that demonstrate the acquisition of skills and knowledge (Brooks and Brooks, 1993).

This shift focusing on how students learn is known as constructivism. Our definition of teaching—changing your behavior to increase the likelihood that students change their behavior—is still applicable in the constructivist model. The difference is that the teacher is now the "guide on the side," designing appropriate learning experiences that help students internalize and integrate new information, thus creating new understanding for themselves (Gardner, 1991), rather than the "sage on the stage" when knowledge is transmitted passively from the teacher to students.

Most teachers still recognize that many times it is important to be the active "sage on the stage," because lower-level foundational knowledge is usually a prerequisite for future understanding and inquiry. Teacher-directed instruction is often quite appropriate. Therefore, we will first describe effective direct instructional teacher behaviors; then various constructivist techniques will be discussed.

Direct Instruction

For lower level cognitive objectives, direct teacher instruction often is the most efficient and effective means of instructional delivery. Research has identified five components of lesson design that are effective in improving student achievement when teachers employ direct instructional methodologies (Hunter, 1982, Rosenshine and Stevens, 1986). These components are entry, input, checking for understanding, providing practice, and closure.

Entry

The first component of a lesson should be an introduction, usually called entry. Here teacher behavior is directed towards gaining student attention and involvement, reviewing past material, and stating what the student will learn.

Attention and involvement is gained by beginning lessons with novel, discrepant, or interesting activities. Some examples include:

→ A sixth grade science teacher pretends to accidentally lean on a fire extinguisher. The explosive release of CO_2 gas causes many students to jump from their seats. Then the teacher states, "Today we will be starting our study of gases."

→ A high school social studies class studying the legal system is shocked in the beginning of class when three prearranged students run into the room and grab the teacher's briefcase. With the students staring in utter disbelief, the teacher acts shocked and extremely nervous and requests that another get the principal. While waiting for the principal to arrive, he asks his students to provide a description of the three students. After getting somewhat of a consensus, he invites the three students back into the room. The description of the students is usually quite dissimilar to their actual appearance. Thus begins a lesson on the validity of eyewitness identification in the criminal justice system.

→ A seventh grade class enters their English classroom. The room is filled with the aroma and sound of popping corn. Each student is provided with a small bag of freshly popped corn. The teacher has the students describe the smells, sounds, and tastes. This is an introduction to descriptive, creative writing.

Another function of entry is bringing prior content to the forefront of student awareness. This is accomplished by reviewing past material. The more students are involved in the review, the more effective is the review. One of the quickest and most effective means is by using openers. Openers are short questions or problems placed on the board or duplicated and passed out that require students to use previously covered material. A side benefit of openers is that students begin to arrive a little earlier to class and settle down to work more quickly.

Finally, students are made aware of the learning objectives of the lesson. The easiest way to accomplish this is by placing an outline on the board or telling the class what they will be learning. Preferably, you should relate the importance of the new learning to students' lives.

Input

Entry is followed by presenting new academic content called input. Learning is enhanced when the presentation is meaningful, organized, and clear.

Content is most meaningful to students when it is connected to prior learning or is related to the students' own experiences. Content is organized when its conceptual structure is made explicit. The use of charts, tables, diagrams, outlines, and flow charts explicitly shows how facts and concepts are related to each other. For example, students often confuse the concepts of geometry: polygons, quadrilaterals, parallelograms, rectangles, squares, and rhombuses. This confusion is often eliminated by a carefully constructed concept map that diagrams the relationships among these concepts. If students are involved in the analysis and design of this concept map, there is an even greater likelihood that they will understand the hierarchical nature of the concepts.

Content has increased clarity when instructional delivery is well-paced, and teachers cue transitions, emphasize important material, provide examples of the content in many different contexts, and avoid confounding the content with extraneous information.

Checking for Understanding

During and following input, teachers need to check for student understanding. This ongoing evaluation answers the important question, "Are the students ready for me to continue?" Checking is most frequently accomplished by observing student seat work or by sampling a cross-section of the class with questions that require understanding for a correct response. This usually means asking questions that require more than one word answers. Effective questioning techniques including wait-time, equal response opportunities, and hierarchical ordering are used to decide if adjustments in input are needed.

Providing Practice

Once the content or academic skill has been presented and understanding has been checked, students are ready to practice their new understandings. Practice starts with the teacher modeling the use of the content or skill. Often the teacher solves a problem at the board, frequently asking for student input as to the next step. The process of thinking out loud where the teacher verbalizes each succeeding step is particularly helpful for students, because it enables the students to hear, as well as to see on the blackboard, the process the teacher is using to solve the problem.

Next, students are provided with coached practice. Students are given problems to practice. This practice is highly supervised with frequent teacher feedback. Once the teacher is certain that the students are experiencing high rates of success, he provides time for the students to practice independently. Retention of new learning is enhanced when opportunities are given to practice not only immediately following the presentation of the new content, but throughout the week, month, and academic year.

Closure

Closure is the opposite of entry. Student attention and involvement are critical in this summary stage. For example, randomly questioning the class or using exit slips during the last few minutes of class requiring all students to answer a few brief questions on the important aspects of the day's lesson allows students to review the day's content.

A special type of exit slip ties the closure of one day's lesson to the introduction of the next day's lesson. The students write what was the most important thing that they learned that day and what questions they still had about the lesson. The students' questions then are used as the openers for the next day's lesson.

Closure also provides students with a brief preview of what new material is yet to be learned. The use of an on-going outline or concept map accomplishes this.

Constructivism

So far, effective instruction has focused on the delivery of lower-level cognitive skills with the teacher being the most important variable in the teaching/learning process. Now we focus on instruction methodology that emphasizes higher-order thinking skills, such as analysis, synthesis, and evaluation, emphasizing how students use these skills to develop new understanding; so the most important variable in the teaching/learning process is now the student.

Unlike direct instruction with its emphasis upon specific teacher behavior, constructivism consists of theoretical models that guide rather than prescribe teacher behavior. The new paradigm is explained and implemented under various models including Teaching for

Understanding (Perkins and Blythe, 1994), Dimensions of Learning (Marzano, 1992), and Multiple Intelligences (Gardner, 1983). The authors believe that the shift in emphasis is accommodated with instructional strategies typically grouped under the heading of authentic instruction.

Theoretically there are five key criteria that distinguish authentic instruction from direct instruction (Newmann and Wehlage, 1993). These are 1) an emphasis on higher-order cognitive skills, 2) a deeper understanding of a fewer number of concepts, 3) connecting classroom activities to the world outside the classroom, 4) complex verbal interactions between teacher and students and between students, and 5) a classroom environment that encourages respect and intellectual risk taking, founded on a belief that all students are capable of learning. In addition, many educators include a sixth criteria, authentic assessment. Authentic assessment involves the integration of the five criteria listed above by requiring students to work through complex relevant problems using their new understanding (Brooks and Brooks, 1993, Schnitzer, 1993). Often students acquire additional new skills and understanding during authentic assessment. Thus authentic assessment is viewed as ongoing instruction and is not separated from instruction, as is the case with traditional paper and pencil tests.

In classroom practice, authentic instruction is the solving of real-world types of problems such as solving solid waste issues of the community, determining the accuracy of National Weather Service forecasts, collecting data for studies conducted by scientists, or doing historical research, rather than the typical textbook type problem sets. As in the real world, problems are usually not well-defined and require the use of many skills and the understanding of many concepts that frequently cross traditional subject matter boundaries. Problems most often are solved by a cooperative team of students, rarely by an individual student. Finally, the solution to the problem, which also serves as the assessment of student learning, is usually a complex product involving position papers, outlines of procedures or policies, or prototype models. It is never a paper and pencil test.

The cognitive justifications for authentic instruction are many, the most important being a deeper understanding of concepts. However the pragmatic justification may actually be more salient, that is, the preparation of students to be competent in the technologically complex, information rich, globally interdependent Twenty-first Century.

Table 6.1 outlines the major differences between direct instruction and constructivism.

TABLE 6.1 *Differences Between Direct Instruction and Constructivism*

DIRECT INSTRUCTION	CONSTRUCTIVISM
students assimilating facts	students understanding concepts
assigning little importance to students' prior experiences and knowledge in their understanding of new learning	assigning major importance to students' prior experiences and knowledge in their understanding of new learning
assessment that requires students to supply a set of correct answers	assessment that requires students to demonstrate their understanding by the display of academic products and the performance of behaviors that require the understanding, integration, and application of concepts
individual student-teacher interaction	interaction of communities of student learners
primarily academic tasks requiring mathematical and verbal abilities	tasks requiring multiple intelligences such as mathematical, linguistic, kinesthetic, musical
academic tasks that are unrelated to the real-life world outside the classroom	academic tasks that reflect and mirror the real-life world outside the classroom

MOTIVATION

It has become the gospel in American education that teachers should reward appropriate student behaviors and punish inappropriate ones. This is intended to reinforce and increase the likelihood that appropriate behavior is repeated and inappropriate behavior is extinguished. These practices follow the principles of operant conditioning (Skinner, 1974) which assume that behavior is determined solely by external consequences. Besides the hotly-debated question as to whether this approach has been successful in our schools (Kohn, 1993), there are many philosophical and psychological misgivings, some of which will be discussed later.

Like direct instruction which places the responsibility of student learning on the teacher, operant conditioning views the teacher as the primary source of student motivation. The focus on the teacher as the source of student motivation is questioned primarily for its assumed lack of importance of the role the student plays in his own motivation. Unlike operant conditioning, social cognitive theory of motivation not only considers external antecedents and consequences of behavior, but also takes into consideration how an individual's beliefs, expectations, and emotions influence his behavior. Similar to the constructivist theory of instruction which places the student at the center of his own knowledge acquisition, the social cognitive theory of motivation places the student at the center of his own motivation. The student, rather than the teacher, is the primary source of motivation. The teacher, rather than distributing praise and rewards or delivering punishments, behaves in ways that encourage the development of the student's intrinsic motivation. In other words, the teacher exhibits behavior that both increases the student's expectation of success through an internal locus of control and that increases the intrinsic value of achievement to the student. Some of the important social cognitive motivational approaches that teachers may employ in classrooms include redefining success, islands of competence, encouragement, feeling tone, interest, and knowledge of results.

Redefining Success

We live in a society which glorifies winners and excoriates losers. "Winning isn't everything. It's the only thing." This axiom, attributed to the late Vince Lombardi coach of the Green Bay Packers of the NFL, works really well on the college or professional football field where the players have exceptional abilities and personal histories full of many individual successes. However, it works very poorly in the classroom where students have a wide range of abilities and variable histories of success. By focusing upon only a very specific level of performance defined as winning, a reward/punishment scenario is created in which very few are rewarded and everyone else is punished by not receiving rewards.

Our society does not value effort as much as result. For example let's take a look at the plight of the Buffalo Bills' football team. They made it to four Super Bowls but each time lost. Was the focus on that this was a great team and significantly better, in fact, than any other pro football team but one? Was credit given to the masterful coaching and heroic play that was needed for this team to arrive at this level? Not at all. The press and the fans treated them as bums. They said, "They choked," and "They didn't have what it took." We have frequently heard, on the playgrounds and in the schools that we visit, students saying that "second place is first loser." With this orientation that winning is the only thing, how can any student who does not "win" maintain a positive expectation of success? They can't.

Teachers who mainly rely on rewards for specific levels of performance foster all out competition where there are few winners and mostly losers. Traditional classroom practices, such as 1) normative grading, 2) calling on the first person to raise his hand, 3) passing out incentives and rewards for the best grades, 4) providing feedback which focuses solely on level of performance (e.g. "Excellent paper! You've received the highest grade in the class."), and 5) making group activities contingent upon individual performance (e.g. "If everyone does well on the test, we'll have a pizza party on Friday."), foster competition and focus attention upon only the highest levels of achievement. This decreases motivation for the majority of students by reducing their expectation of success.

Teachers need to communicate to students that they are in competition with themselves, not with other students. Teachers increase motivation when increasing the individual's expectation of success by using classroom practices that decrease competition and focus attention upon student effort. Examples of such practices include: 1) assessing by criterion referenced evaluation, 2) using wait time to maximize the possibility that all students formulate an answer, 3) significantly reducing the use of incentives and rewards for the best grades, 4) providing feedback which emphasizes effort (e.g. "It's apparent to me that you put more effort into this paper."), and 5) making group activities independent of individual performance (e.g. "We're having a pizza party on Friday.").

Teachers can concentrate their positive attention upon incremental achievement. This is another way of affirming and encouraging effort. The student's efforts, no matter how minor, ought to be affirmed as long as they are in the desired direction, and/or it represents a change from his previous level of achievement.

For example, if you have been encouraging a student who does no homework to try harder and finally this student comes into class with a wadded up piece of paper and throws it on your desk, is this a success? Insofar as it does advance the student in the desired direction and represents a change in activity level, it is a true success. This tiny ember of success can be snuffed out by proving to the student that nothing he does is good enough. A student may ask, "Why try?" to a comment such as "I don't accept homework that looks like this." On the other hand it can be nurtured and fanned into a flame, thereby increasing the likelihood of future successes with a comment such as, "I have a problem. My problem is that you have put some effort into this assignment. I want to be certain that I can read it accurately, but I'm not sure that I can because of its condition. I will do my best with this. Please try not to crumple it tomorrow."

When success is redefined not as certain performance but as effort, we increase the possibility that all students can experience significant success. Individuals can always put forth more effort. It is not enough, however, to tell a student to "try harder." It may be overwhelming to a student who repeatedly fails to tell him to "just try harder." What is needed is the recognition of the effort when it is displayed by the student.

Islands of Competence

In addition to redefining success, another way to increase student motivation by increasing students' success/failure ratio is to recognize the students' "islands of competence." Robert Brooks, an authority on student self-esteem, emphasizes this concept in his work with difficult students, especially those with ADHD (1991). "Island of competence" refers to the time-honored idea that everyone is good at something or as Brooks states, "one area that is or has the potential to be a source of pride and achievement" (1991, p. 31). Sometimes the competence is readily apparent, as when a student is very interested in animals and has knowledge concerning their habits and care. Other times competence is apparent, but the teacher believes it has no relationship to learning goals, such as the student who produces elaborate artistic doodles rather than finishing the assigned task. Still, other times it is not readily apparent and is ascertained only by careful interviewing by the teacher; such as when a teacher in a northern Minnesota school asks a child in his class about his hobbies and finds out that he collects and knows a lot about tropical seashells. Finally, sometimes competence is masked and needs to be extrapolated and reframed from student behavior, such as viewing hyperactivity as high energy rather than merely disruptive behavior. When high energy is channeled into appropriate classroom tasks, it may lead to many areas of student competency, which otherwise goes unnoticed.

When you identify a student's island of competence, you then can build success by helping him use his competency by designing tasks which directly relate to the student's island of competence or by showing the student how his competency may be applied to the learning activity. In other words, providing a student with opportunities to do what he's good at, increases the likelihood of his success thus beginning the cycle of high motivation discussed in Chapter 4. This may mean allowing the student interested in animals to be responsible for the care of the class' aquarium, to teach fellow students and teachers about the care and feeding of animals, or to write about animals. It may also mean that the teacher intentionally integrates the subject of animals into the class' study of art, science, math, or history.

Rewards and Encouragement

In the last chapter when coercive authority was discussed, it was pointed out that such authority relies upon the teacher dispensing rewards and punishments. This method of student management is firmly grounded in the principles of operant conditioning. However, earlier in this chapter we stated that there has been a move away from operant conditioning toward a social cognitive theory of motivation. Therefore, in this section we first discuss the problem with rewards and then detail an alternative technique, encouragement, which is more congruent with the social cognitive theory of motivation.

Problems with Rewards

Since reward giving is so ingrained in many teachers' motivational strategies, we have decided to discuss why wholesale reward giving must be rejected. What is the effect of rewards upon the motivation of students? What is the message when a student is given a sticker or cookie? Does the student get the message that he is a competent able individual? Alfie Kohn (1993) states rewards are forms of control. They convey little to the student other than that he has conformed to our expectations and we are pleased. The student enjoys the cookie and the positive feeling lasts as long as it takes to eat that cookie. Motivation for future projects is therefore controlled by the size and type of the cookie, the student's present desire for a cookie, and/or the student's desire to please the teacher. Each of the above is an extrinsic motivator which fosters extrinsic motivation, which is contrary to our stated goal of increasing intrinsic motivation.

We seriously question whether the average teacher really wishes to send the message that the reason to study long division is to receive a snack. Most teachers tell us that the reward is meant only as a means to the desired end of getting students to master material. They believe that once the material is mastered, the student will continue to be motivated for intrinsic reasons rather than rewards. For example, reading programs often reward students for each book they read. The reasoning is that once the student learns to read and recognizes the pleasure reading brings, rewards are unnecessary. However, it is most often the case that when rewards are withdrawn, the incidence of reading decreases drastically. In fact, in order to restimulate reading behavior, larger rewards are frequently required. This is because extrinsic motivation decreases intrinsic motivation.

One explanation of this phenomenon is due to the "discounting principle" (Morgan, 1984). The discounting principle states that people tend to discount alternative explanations for their behavior if another explanation is more salient. Thus when a student believes that the purpose of reading a book is to gain a highly evident reward, then he will not attribute his reading behavior to pleasure which is a far less salient explanation. Therefore a young student may refuse to read any more books, because he already has more stickers than anyone else in the class. In an older student, where the belief may be that the goal of mastery is to get a good grade, he may refuse to put any additional effort into a task once he is reasonably assured of obtaining the grade he desires.

Some of the drawbacks of rewards are:

→ Rewards are mechanistic. They do not respect the individual's thoughts, feelings, expectations, or perceptions. The student is dealt with as an animal in a "Skinner Box," a device for training animals, mostly rodents, named after the late B.F. Skinner, the father of operant conditioning. As Arthur Koestller (1967) says: "For the anthropomorphic view of the rat, American Psychology substituted a rattomorphic view of man."

→ Ascertaining appropriate rewards and punishments becomes increasingly more difficult as students get older.

→ Rewards may reduce an individual's willingness to do more than what is expected. The student has a tendency, if behavior is contingency based, to perform only as much as is needed to receive a reward. Extra effort is thereby discouraged.

→ Behaviors are evidenced only under conditions of rewards. This partially explains why behaviors evidenced under conditions of rewards don't generalize to other situations. If the teacher reduces the intrinsic motives for student behavior by paying for performance, a student is apt to reason, "Why should I work for free?"

→ Rewards are available only to the winners, that is, to a few individuals. Therefore, rewards create quitters. By only rewarding certain performance, rewards guarantee that those individuals who feel or indeed are unable to meet the mark, quit.

→ Rewards create dependency. If student behavior is rewarded by the teacher, then the student becomes dependent upon the teacher for motivation.

→ Rewards discourage risk-taking behavior, stifle creativity, and decrease the opportunity for students to construct new knowledge. If the focus of the activity is to gain a reward, then any behaviors which do not move directly towards the goal tend to be discouraged. This encourages students to find the quickest, easiest way to achieve the task at hand.

→ Rewards foster competition and thus discourage cooperative learning. If only a few rewards are available, why would one student want to voluntarily help another student and thus increase the competition for the reward.

A particular type of reward, praise, demonstrates all of these drawbacks. Since praise feels so good to the sender and is so easy to use, it is particularly difficult to understand why praise causes problems. Many readers possibly are saying to themselves, "Now you've gone too far! My students, especially the difficult ones, need more praise not less!"

If you tell a student, "You have done a good job," what are you really communicating to that student? You are pleased and the student has met your criteria for reward. Is pleasing you really your intended goal, or is it the student's feeling of accomplishment which is important? With praise the student tends to becomes less intrinsically motivated for all the drawbacks associated with rewards.

So, should teachers never provide rewards to students? It would be unrealistic for us to suppose that you, upon reading this book, will suddenly cease rewarding or praising students. What is more realistic is that you can learn to couple rewards with messages that are performance/content specific. You can, in other words, provide verbal feedback to the student about the positive degree of competence and effort, not just that the student did a "good job" (Rosenfield et al., 1980). "I can see that you put a lot of effort into this project and demonstrated your understanding of the concepts. You have earned a B"; not "Good Job! Here's what you've won!" More importantly, if you feel that you must reward a student or group, there is reason to believe that the less expected the reward is, the less problematic. It is when the task is performed in order to obtain the reward that most difficulties arise. Unexpected rewards may be quite exciting and pleasant.

Encouragement

Of course the obvious next question is, "If I lessen my use of rewards because of its often deleterious effects, with what should I replace it?" The authors believe that the use of encouragement is very valuable. We define encouragement as any teacher behavior that focuses students' attention on effort, their capabilities, their interests, or the relevance and usefulness of any task or behavior. The purpose of encouragement is to increase the likelihood that students develop an internal locus of control and internal value structure in order to increase intrinsic motivation.

The following are the characteristics of encouragement.

→ Encouragement focuses on effort.
→ Encouragement is available to all, not just to those who achieve at the highest levels.
→ Encouragement creates triers because increased effort leads to increased success which increases motivation.
→ Encouragement is congruent with the student's innate desire to develop mastery (White, 1959).
→ Encouragement inspires independence. By focusing upon internal motivators, the student is less dependent upon the teacher for motivation.
→ Encouragement increases cooperation among students by decreasing competition for limited rewards.
→ Encouragement increases the likelihood that new behavior generalizes, because the students' focus is upon the newly acquired skill and not upon an external reward.
→ Encouragement increases the risk-taking of learners and therefore the possibility of students' constructing new knowledge because the focus is upon effort and not certain outcome.
→ Encouragement is equally effective at any age.

For the reader who may now be questioning the use of rewards, we refer to Kohn (1993) for a more thorough discussion of the topic.

Feeling Tone

Feeling tone has to do with the emotional feel of a classroom and is commonly referred to as the classroom climate or classroom atmosphere. Your non-verbal and verbal behavior in the classroom establishes the feeling tone in your classes (Withall, 1969). As stated throughout this book, the beliefs a teacher holds about students in general, and individual students in particular, greatly influence the behavior of the teacher. Of particular importance for student motivation are teacher beliefs about student ability and willingness to learn. These beliefs are commonly referred to as teacher expectations for student achievement.

If a teacher has different expectations for each student, the teacher behaves differently toward each student; thus each student perceives a different classroom climate. For example, teachers who view certain students as low achievers commonly communicate lower expectations to these students than they communicate to students whom they view as high achievers. Teachers communicate their lower expectations of some students to them by 1) calling on them less often to answer questions, 2) using less wait time, 3) asking a greater number of lower level questions, 4) expressing less personal interest, and 5) standing farther away.

Such behaviors establish a discouraging classroom climate by sending a powerful message to these students, "I don't expect you to do well in this class." This message encourages students to develop low expectations of success, and therefore they put less effort into academic tasks. If a student performs poorly, it reinforces the teacher's low expectations and intensifies the differential treatment of the student (Braun, 1976). Having low expectations for students sets up the following process. The teacher thinks, "Why should I try? He will not succeed," and the student thinks, "Why should I try? I will not succeed."

Some readers may be thinking that it may be important to treat lower achievers differently so as to not embarrass them or to give them unrealistic expectations for future success. However, when success is redefined as legitimate effort, then all students can achieve success. Teachers enhance the probability that all students are more intrinsically motivated when they have the expectation that all students can be successful and communicate this through the use of encouragement,

Interest

Intrinsic motivation is facilitated when students are interested in what they are learning. When students are interested, they have an internal value structure. How can you facilitate your students' interest? One very effective way is the use of discrepant events. Students, like all people, are naturally curious, having an innate tendency to explore (Kagan, 1972). This innate curiosity can be piqued when discrepant events are used in instruction. A discrepant event is any experience that varies from expectations or closely held beliefs.

A frequently used discrepant event in elementary science education is what's called the "floating rock" demonstration. In this demonstration, the teacher has a water filled aquarium and an object that looks like a rock. He asks the class what will happen if he places the rock into the aquarium, and naturally all the students agree, from past experience, that the rock will sink to the bottom of the aquarium. When he places the rock in the aquarium, instead of sinking, it floats. For the students, this forms a discrepancy between what they anticipated would happen and what in fact happened. The students are very interested in now exploring the reasons why this rock floats.

An example from high school social studies involves what students believe about Christopher Columbus. The teacher starts by asking students to list what they know about Christopher Columbus. The list most probably includes such "facts" as he was a friend of the Indians, he was a kind man, he was the first to discover the New World, and he brought back spices and gold to Spain. The teacher then reads the following description of how Columbus obtained gold from the Indians:

> Every man and woman, every boy or girl of fourteen or older . . . had to collect gold for the Spaniards. As their measure, the Spaniards used hawks' bells. Every three months every Indian had to bring to one of the forts a hawks' bell filled with gold dust. The chiefs had to bring in about ten times that amount . . .
>
> . . . Copper tokens were manufactured, and when an Indian had brought his or her tribute to an armed post, he or she received such a token, stamped with the month, to be hung around

the neck. With that they were safe for another three months while collecting more gold. Whoever was caught without a token was killed by having his or her hands cut off . . . There were no gold fields, and thus, once the Indians had handed in whatever they still had in gold ornaments, their only hope was to work all day in the streams, washing out gold dust from the pebbles. It was an impossible task, but those Indians that tried to flee into the mountains were systematically hunted down with dogs and killed . . . Thus it was at this time that the mass suicides began: the Arawaks killed themselves with cassava poison. During those two years of the administration of the brothers Columbus, an estimated one half of the entire population of Hispaniola was killed or killed themselves. The estimates run from 125,000 to one-half million." (Bigelow, 1991, p. 258).

This passage challenges students' commonly held beliefs and is, like the floating rock, a discrepant event. In both examples, the discrepancy creates what is called cognitive dissonance, that is, an anxiety caused by the difference between what is observed and what students believe or have experienced in the past. When this dissonance exists, students are intrinsically motivated to relieve the anxiety. In the classroom, dissonance is resolved by investigating the discrepancy in more depth and thus increasing students' understanding and knowledge.

A more general way to increase student interest is to ensure that the lessons are relevant. Student interest is always enhanced when the students perceive the relevancy of what they are learning to their lives. This emphasizes the importance of providing students both with the rationale for various learning activities and with planning activities that reflect real life situations (Stipek, 1993), thus using authentic instruction.

Knowledge of Results

Imagine this situation. You are a participant in a classroom demonstration and are asked to toss a tennis ball into a trash can while you are blindfolded. The teacher supplies tennis balls and you start tossing. How long will you be motivated to continue tossing the balls? If you are like the many teachers whom we have asked to volunteer for this demonstration, you'll be ready to call it quits probably after four or five unsuccessful tosses. The reason is the successful completion of the task, that is, getting the ball in the can, is almost impossible under these circumstances. The expectation of success is therefore close to nil. If a participant is successful, it is a function of luck, not of effort or competence.

What is needed to increase the expectation of success? You need direct, descriptive feedback. This feedback is called knowledge of results. Knowledge of results is not judgmental or evaluative such as "good job" or "you're doing great." It is descriptive, providing the learner with the knowledge needed to increase the possibility of attaining the goal. This knowledge consists of informing the student of what is done correctly, what needs to be changed, and in some cases, how to affect the change.

Going back to the ball tossing demonstration, suppose at the time you were ready to quit, the teacher started to give you specific feedback on your tosses. For example, you toss the ball, and the teacher says, "More to the left." After the next toss, he says, "That's the right direction. Now toss it about 2 feet longer." How long do you think that it would take you to put the ball in the basket? It is our experience that under these feedback conditions, success is achieved in less than five tosses.

Initially when the tosses occur randomly without the knowledge of results, the expectation of success is dependent upon luck and therefore low, and the locus of control is external.

However when the teacher begins to provide specific feedback, the attribution for success is shifted inward, and competence and effort determine whether the participant is successful. At this point the expectation of success is high; the locus of control is internal, and therefore the motivation moves from extrinsic to intrinsic.

One way that knowledge of results may be communicated is through criterion referenced evaluation. Criterion referenced evaluation clearly delineates what needs to be done to successfully complete a task. In contrast, how many times does a student receive a paper back from a teacher with the only comment on it, "good job but needs some additional work," and a grade marked as a big red C+. How do you think the student feels? Does the student have an understanding of exactly what additional work is needed? Does the teacher indicate that he recognizes how much effort the student put into the paper, or that the opening paragraph is a real attention getter? What about that impressive bibliography? Does the teacher let the student know that the teacher notices how far back the student went to get those obscure articles? What effect is this type of feedback and evaluation likely to have upon the student's future expectation of success? How much time and effort is the student likely to dedicate to the next report?

An alternative to the above manner of evaluating projects with random comments and an assigned final grade is to use a criterion referenced evaluation format. This requires that an academic task be analyzed into its component parts. For example, instead of a research paper being viewed as a single piece of work, it is viewed as a product of many academic skills. One teacher's analysis of the academic components needed to be included in a research paper includes: topic selection, source cards, preliminary outline, final outline, paragraph development, bibliography, rough draft, and final copy.

Next, each of these component parts is itself analyzed with the intent of delineating both the subcomponents and a description of the various levels of performance for each subcomponent. For example, the same teacher divides the component of paragraph development into two subcomponents, content and format and describes various levels of performance along a continuum, as shown below.

Paragraph Development

Content

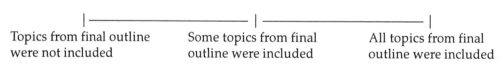

| Topics from final outline were not included | Some topics from final outline were included | All topics from final outline were included |

This type of analysis is continued until all the main components of the research project are listed with subcomponents and performance criteria.

By analyzing a final product into subcomponents, teachers are recognizing that every student is not competent in every academic area but is competent in some areas. For example, a teacher is saying in a criterion referenced evaluation of a specific student, "Taylor you may not be the best in grammar, but you are excellent in finding sources of information and you are recognized for that." Thus, the teacher is increasing opportunities for success.

Criterion referenced evaluation also provides students with the opportunity to evaluate their own work, which has been shown in one study to significantly improve academic achievement (Levin and Heath, 1981).

Criterion referenced evaluation when designed and used to 1) eliminate the ambiguity of an academic task and thus reduce the perceived difficulty of the task (Stipek, 1993), 2) have students set personal goals (Stipek, 1993), 3) maximize the opportunities for success, and 4) provide opportunities for self-evaluation (Bandura, 1986), increases the probability that students move from an external locus of control to an internal locus of control and therefore are intrinsically motivated.

SELF-ESTEEM

Recall that in previous chapters self-esteem was defined as the sum of significance, competence, virtue, and power, $SE = S + C + V + P$, and it is either pro-social or distorted. Upon reflection it now hopefully is apparent to you, the reader, that what has already been detailed about the prevention of discipline problems, specifically effective instruction and motivation, has significant effects upon students' pro-social self-esteem.

Competence and Power

Effective instruction impacts the pro-social self-esteem of students through the components of competence and power. The entire focus of effective instruction is to increase the probability that students are successful or competent. With increased success comes an increase in the success/failure ratio which in turn leads to a greater expectation of future success or motivation, which in turn leads to increased effort. This cycle of increasingly higher motivation leads to the student's perception that he has the ability to change things in his environment in a manner that he desires, which is the definition of power.

Social cognitive approaches to motivation also impact the pro-social self-esteem of students through the components of competence and power. The entire focus of motivation is to increase student effort. With increased effort comes an increase in success or competence which in turn increases the success/failure ratio, which in turn produces a higher expectation for future success or greater motivation. This again illustrates the cycle of high motivation (review Figure 4.1).

Social cognitive motivational approaches foster students' intrinsic motivation. The importance of intrinsic motivation is that when faced with challenges, students with intrinsic motivation are likely to put forth greater effort in pursuit of their goals. Consequently they experience more successes and thus feel even more competent. In addition, because they have learned that it is their effort and ability and not luck, degree of difficulty, or how much they are being paid which determines their ultimate success, they feel powerful.

Significance

"I don't care how much you know until I know how much you care." This sentiment expressed by a student sums up the difficulties that a history of negative interactions causes for the relationship of the student and the teacher. If he comes into your classroom with a history of being demeaned, berated, and generally disliked by teachers, you have your work cut out for you. It first is necessary to show this student that you have respect and positive regard for him. But how can you authentically do this? To begin, you may use accurate empathy with the child (see Chapter 1). What would you want, given a history similar to this student, in order to feel cared about and to care in return? Most probably you would want a significant amount of trust, kindness, respect for your individuality and autonomy, and a clear indication that someone liked you, cared about you, and valued you. Therefore this is what your student, in all likelihood, also needs and will respond to positively. Are you able to demonstrate these affective behaviors toward your difficult students? To the extent that you find something to legitimately like about each of these students, you increase the likelihood that you will be able to provide your difficult students with positive regard.

Much like islands of competence, we all have "islands of significance;" that is, there is something to like in all students. Sometimes you have to look beyond the student's defensiveness and aggressive posturing. If you wish to be effective in increasing the probability that your student feels more significant, you must find something to like about every student in your class. Only if you find something you like, will you be able to interact honestly with the student in a positive and authentically caring fashion. The only thing that you may find to like about a student initially is his tenacity of his distorted beliefs and behaviors. Think what gains the student may achieve if his tenacity is focused in another direction. You can be the teacher to increase the probability of that occurring.

Any time you talk to the student in a positive manner, especially if it is casual and not related to academics, you increase the likelihood that the student feels more significant. When we ask teachers to remember when they were students and recall experiences that made them feel good about themselves, almost without exception they relate non-academic positive interactions with teachers. They give responses such as the following, "My teacher came up to me and said I had a very nice smile." "One day, for factors having nothing to do with school, I was feeling very down. That evening my teacher called my house and asked me how I was doing." Calling home to chat, sending postcards from trips, inquiring about out of school activities, talking to students about their special interests, remembering birthdays, and acknowledging special family events all increase a student's sense of significance. "Most positive school experiences have nothing to do with academics; they have to do with personal relationships that take less than five seconds of time" (Brooks, 1995).

You may now be agreeing with us that interacting with students in a manner designed to increase their pro-social significance is important and necessary. However, we must warn you about a formidable obstacle to successfully intervening with chronically disruptive students, including those with ADHD, in this manner. Many of these students feel so defective and inadequate that they view with suspicion any adult who seems to value them. To protect their self-esteem they act defensively and with hostility. Expressions of positive regard by the teacher create cognitive dissonance in the minds of students who are used to being rejected. As explained before, this dissonance needs to be resolved. One way for the student to resolve it is for him to accept the teacher's valuation. However, this is at odds with the student's belief of not being valued, as well as his prior negative experiences with teachers. It is far easier to resolve this dissonance by rejecting the honest approaches and person of the teacher, which increases the probability that the teacher, in turn, will reject him. Thus the student's world view is confirmed.

To get past this defensive posture requires the teacher to have tenacity and patience. "Relationship building is an endurance event" (Brendtro et al., 1990, p. 65).

Virtue

Virtue, as previously defined, is a person's perceived feeling of worthiness as a result of his ability and willingness to help others. While everyone has the ability to help someone else, willingness is a factor of caring about others. The teacher who desires to enhance a student's sense of pro-social virtue must not only provide opportunities for the student to display virtue, but must also increase the likelihood that the student cares about the teacher and the class.

If the student does not care about you, if the student does not feel affiliated with the class, or if he feels alienated from the school, he will not be inclined to display virtue with these groups. He will instead display virtue by helping another group with which he is affiliated. If this is a group of troublemakers, watch out.

When teachers help students feel more significant, they help these students to begin to care about themselves and the class and so lay the foundation for future virtuous behavior.

Once students feel a sense of significance and so are willing to be virtuous, teachers must provide the opportunities for the student to display virtue, such as encouraging them to help classmates or younger students with school activities including academics, sports, and hobbies. Other examples of opportunities to display virtue include helping teachers prepare for back to school night, setting up their bulletin boards, cleaning closets, passing out supplies, and assisting with the myriad of other teacher activities in which students may be legitimately supportive. Some recently developed programs such as peer mediation or peer listening provide excellent opportunities for students to become engaged in virtuous behavior. Some schools have moved beyond the school building into the community in attempting to give students broader opportunities for the development of pro-social virtue by instituting service learning. Volunteering time in community organizations and services not only benefits the community as a whole, but seems to also have positive effects on students' sense of virtue.

A cautionary note is that if students perceive that they are being coerced or compelled to help others by tying virtuous behavior to grades, consequences, or rewards, the positive effect of these opportunities may be lost because of the discounting principle. The positive feelings of worthiness experienced by students involved in virtuous behavior are the goals that teachers need to emphasize.

SUMMARY

This chapter considered how teachers may prevent disruptive student behavior by increasing students' success/failure ratios and facilitating the development of intrinsic motivation and prosocial self-esteem. This is primarily accomplished by teachers focusing on effective instruction, motivation, and other behaviors intended to enhance students' prosocial significance and virtue.

Effective instruction is divided into direct instruction and constructivism. Direct instruction focuses on the behavior of teachers related to improving student academic achievement in the lower levels of the cognitive domain. Effective direct instruction involves the five lesson components of entry, input, checking for understanding, providing practice, and closure. Constructivism focuses upon the student as a learner of higher order cognitive skills. The model of authentic instruction was used to explain the differences that exist between direct instruction and constructivism.

The focus of effective instruction is on increasing students' success/failure ratio. This increase in success results in more effort or motivation which further increases success, thus impacting the pro-social self-esteem of students through the components of competence and power.

The motivation theory of operant conditioning and social cognition were contrasted. Social cognitive techniques of redefining success, islands of competency, encouragement, interest, and knowledge of results facilitate students' internal locus of control and therefore effort. As with effective instruction, motivation, especially intrinsic motivation, enhances pro-social self-esteem through the components of competence and power.

Teachers also facilitate the development of pro-social significance by using accurate empathy, islands of significance, and encouragement. The concept of cognitive dissonance helps explain why some disruptive students are resistant to teachers' attempts to intervene using pro-social significance, and teachers must work hard to overcome this resistance. Finally, teachers also facilitate students' pro-social virtue first by enhancing students' sense that they are cared about and then by providing students opportunities to display virtuous behavior.

Concept Map

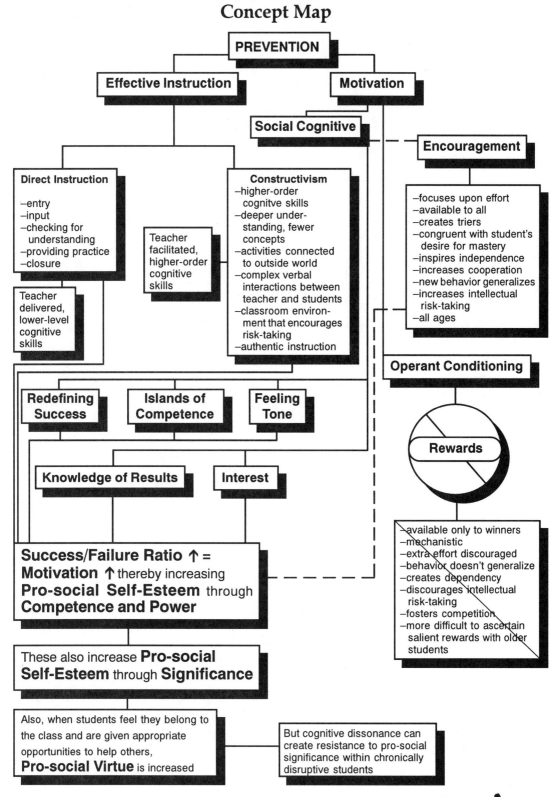

PREVENTION

Effective Instruction

Motivation

Social Cognitive

Encouragement

Direct Instruction

–entry
–input
–checking for understanding
–providing practice
–closure

Teacher delivered, lower-level cognitive skills

Teacher facilitated, higher-order cognitive skills

Constructivism
–higher-order cognitve skills
–deeper under-standing, fewer concepts
–activities connected to outside world
–complex verbal interactions between teacher and students
–classroom environ-ment that encourages risk-taking
–authentic instruction

–focuses upon effort
–available to all
–creates triers
–congruent with student's desire for mastery
–inspires independence
–increases cooperation
–new behavior generalizes
–increases intellectual risk-taking
–all ages

Operant Conditioning

Redefining Success

Islands of Competence

Feeling Tone

Rewards

Knowledge of Results

Interest

–available only to winners
–mechanistic
–extra effort discouraged
–behavior doesn't generalize
–creates dependency
–discourages intellectual risk-taking
–fosters competition
–more difficult to ascertain salient rewards with older students

Success/Failure Ratio ↑ = Motivation ↑ thereby increasing **Pro-social Self-Esteem** through **Competence and Power**

These also increase **Pro-social Self-Esteem** through **Significance**

Also, when students feel they belong to the class and are given appropriate opportunities to help others, **Pro-social Virtue** is increased

But cognitive dissonance can create resistance to pro-social significance within chronically disruptive students

REFERENCES

Bandura, A. (1986). *Social Foundations of Thought and Action: Social Cognitive Theory*. Englewood Cliffs, NJ: Prentice Hall.

Bigelow, B. (1991). Columbus in the classroom. from H. Koning, *Columbus: His Enterprise: Exploring the Myth*.

Braun, C. Model of teacher expectations cycle. *Review of Educational Research, 46*, 2, 185-213.

Brendtro, L. K., Brokenleg, M., and Van Bockern, S. (1990). *Reclaiming Youth at Risk: Our Hope for the Future*. Bloomington, IN: National Education Service.

Brooks, R. (1995). *Managing challenging behaviors in children with ADD: It takes two to tango!* Paper presented at Ch.A.D.D. 7th National Convention , Washington, D.C..

Brooks, R. (1991). *The Self-Esteem Teacher*. Circle Pines, MN: American guidance Service.

Brooks, J. G. and Brooks, M. G. (1993). *The Case for Constructivist Classrooms*. Alexandria, VA: Association for Supervision and Curriculum Development.

Brophy, J. E. (1988a). Educating teachers about managing classrooms and students. *Teaching and Teacher Education, 4*, 1, 1-18.

Brophy, J. E. (1988b). Research on teacher effects and abuses. *Elementary School Journal, 89*, 1, 3-21.

Copple, C., Sigel, I., and Saunders, R. (1984). *Educating the Young Thinker*. New York: Van Nostrand.

Dewey, J. (1938). *Experience and Education*. New York: Macmillan.

Gardner, H. (1991). *The Unschooled Mind: How Children Think and How Schools Should Teach*. New York: Basic Books.

Gardner, H. (1983). *Frames of Mind: The Theory of Multiple Intelligences*. New York: Basic Books.

Hunter, M. (1982). *Mastery Teaching*. El Segundo, CA: TIP Publications.

Jackson, P. W. (1986*). The Practice of Teaching*. New York: Teachers College Press.

Kagan, J. (1972). Motives and development. *Journal of Personality and Social Psychology, 22*, 51-66.

Koestler, A. (1967). *The Act of Creation*. New York: Dell.

Kohn, A. (1993). *Punished by Rewards*. Boston: Houghton Mifflin.

Levin, J., and Heath, R. (1981). *Criteria referenced evaluation: Its effect on student achievement, on task behavior and teacher behavior*. Paper presented at the Annual Conference of the Pennsylvania Association for Supervision and Curriculum Development, Harrisburg.

Marzano, R. J. (1992). *A Different Kind of Classroom: Teaching with Dimensions of Learning*. Alexandria, VA: Association for Supervision and Curriculum Development.

Morgan, M. (1984). Rewards-induced decrements and increments in intrinsic motivation. *Review of Educational Research, 54*, 5-30.

Newmann, F. and Wehlage, G. (1993). Five standards of authentic instruction. *Educational Leadership, 50*, 7, 8-12.

Perkins, D. and Blythe, T. (1994). Putting understanding up front. *Educational Leadership, 51*, 5, 4-7.

Piaget, J. and Inhelder, B. (1971). *The Psychology of the Child*. New York: Basic Books.

Rosenfield, D., Folger, R., and Adelman, H. (1980). When rewards reflect competence: A qualification of the over-justification effect. *Journal of Personality and Social Psychology, 39*, 368-376.

Rosenshine, B. and Stevens, R. (1986). Teaching functions. In M. C. Wittrock (Ed.), *Handbook of Research on Teaching*, 3rd. ed. New York: Macmillan.

Schnitzer, S. (1993). Designing an authentic assessment. *Educational Leadership, 50I, 7*, 32-35.

Sigel, I. E. and Cocking, R. R. (1977). *Cognitive Development from Childhood to Adolescence: A Constructivist Perspective*. New York: Holt, Rinehart and Winston.

Skinner, B. F. (1974). *About Behaviorism*. New York: Knopf.

Stipek, D. J. (1993). *Motivation to Learn, From Theory to Practice*, 2nd ed. Boston: Allyn and Bacon.

von Glasersfeld, E. (1981). The concepts of adaptation and viability in radical constructivist theory of knowledge. In , I. E. Sigel, Brodinsky, and Golinkoff (eds.), *New Directions in Piagetian Theory and Practice*. Hillside, NJ: Lawrence Erlbaum Associates.

White, R. (1959). Motivation reconsidered: The concept of competence. *Psychological Review, 66*, 297-333.

Withall, J. (1969). Evaluation of classroom climate. *Childhood Education, 45, 7*, 403-408.

FREQUENTLY ASKED QUESTIONS

1. Researchers invariably rely upon achievement tests to measure effective teaching. Is effective teaching then defined as the number of questions an "effectively taught" student can answer on an objective test?

2. I've always believed that praising students was important. How can I change this practice overnight? Won't this confuse my students?

3. If teachers are to develop their lessons according to the cognitive stage of their students, what happens when there are students from different levels in the same classroom?

4. If I redefine success as effort and not results, am I not doing students a disservice by ill preparing them for the reality of life?

5. "I've got 120 students through my class several times each week. I can't reasonably be expected to write detailed comments on each kid's project or homework. Why isn't it enough to know what grade you got, and what was wrong and right?"

6. Is it okay to do away with homework?

7. If I don't like a student, should I have him removed from my class so that maybe he can gain significance from someone else?

Chapter 7

When Prevention Isn't Enough: The Management of Disruptive Student Behavior by Nonverbal and Verbal Interventions

INTRODUCTION

It is a fact of teaching that no matter how much teachers increase opportunities for student success through effective teaching, facilitate intrinsic motivation in students, and promote students' pro-social self-esteem, some discipline problems still occur. When discipline problems occur, the challenge to the teacher is how to intervene in a manner which encourages continued positive growth in these three domains while at the same time restores appropriate student behavior. To the extent that these interventions are pre-planned and systematic, rather than shooting from the hip and arbitrary, the probability that these interventions will be effective in ending disruptive behavior before it escalates is increased.

This chapter is the first of three chapters concerning management of disruptive behavior. They provide you with a pre-planned hierarchy of coping skills (Levin and Nolan, 1996). The portion of the hierarchy presented in this chapter begins with the least intrusive interventions, nonverbal, and moves toward more intrusive, verbal interventions. These nonverbal and verbal interventions were shown in one study to effectively manage 75 percent of classroom incidents reported by teachers (Shrigley, 1985). Chapters 8 and 9 continue through the hierarchy by exploring interventions designed to manage effectively the remaining 25 percent of behaviors.

GUIDELINES FOR INTERVENTION

Before discussing specific intervention strategies, it is necessary to provide intervention guidelines. These guidelines are designed to ensure that teachers intervene in a manner which does not increase a student's sense of failure, preserves intrinsic motivation by encouraging an internal locus of control, and maintains pro-social self-esteem.

Any effective teacher intervention must:

1. provide the student with the maximum opportunity for controlling his behavior in appropriate ways,

2. not be more disruptive to the class than the student's behavior,
3. decrease the likelihood of a confrontation with the student,
4. protect the physical and psychological safety of the student, the class, and herself, and
5. leave open the greatest number of opportunities for further intervention.

The first guideline addresses a philosophy that has been stated throughout the book, that people can control only their own behavior. By providing the maximum opportunity for students to use this control in an appropriate fashion, teachers are communicating respect for student choice, competence, and power. This increases the possibility of student success in self-management, thereby increasing intrinsic motivation and positively influencing pro-social self-esteem.

The second guideline ensures that the teacher does not become the discipline problem (see Chapter 1) and also recognizes the rights of the other students in the classroom and the teacher's responsibility to them. Although the total hierarchy includes some very confrontational techniques, the very presence of a hierarchical structure is to help you manage behavior in the least confrontational manner possible. If the teacher uses strategies that are more confrontational than needed to encourage student compliance, she is likely to become the discipline problem.

Protecting the physical safety of all students and the teacher herself ought to be the highest priority at all times. Protecting the psychological safety of not only the disruptive student but all students in the class is no less important. Teachers need to analyze empathetically any technique or intervention in order to determine its potential impact upon a student's sense of self-worth. If the intervention demeans, condescends, or attacks the student, then it also decreases the success/failure ratio, intrinsic motivation, and pro-social self-esteem and ought to be scrupulously avoided.

It is often the case that the teacher's first intervention does not result in the desired behavior change. It is important that she then has many more interventions in her repertoire. Using a hierarchical approach guarantees that the teacher still has options for intervention after the first interaction with the disruptive student.

NONVERBAL INTERVENTIONS

It is axiomatic that nonverbal techniques afford the maximum opportunity for students to control themselves. Nonverbal techniques are always less disruptive than the student behavior. They are the least confrontational, and they leave open to the teacher the maximum number of future interventions.

In order to increase effectiveness, nonverbal techniques must be consciously applied in a pre-planned fashion. The teacher skilled in the use of nonverbal techniques uses them in a manner that preserves the privacy and dignity of the disruptive student. They serve as a private message between teacher and student that it is time for the student to use self-control to bring his disruptive behavior into appropriate limits. The teacher uses these nonverbal techniques without interrupting the flow of her lesson. Nonverbal signals are broadly classified as, 1) planned ignoring, 2) signal interference, 3) proximity interference, and 4) touch. These categories are hierarchical as to the degree of possible confrontation.

Planned Ignoring

Planned ignoring is not looking at, recognizing, or in any other manner reacting to a student's disruptive behavior. This does not mean that the teacher is not monitoring the disruptive behavior; it means the teacher has made a conscious decision to ignore the behavior. The rationale for this decision is that by denying the student an opportunity to display distorted power and competence through his disruptive behavior, the teacher increases the likelihood that the student will choose more appropriate behavior. When more appropriate behavior occurs, the teacher ceases ignoring the student and treats the student as she treats all students who are actively involved in the lesson.

For example, a teacher handing out test papers walks by and ignores Bruce and Danny while they are talking and hands out papers to all the other students who are exhibiting appropriate test taking behavior. When Bruce and Danny stop talking, thus bringing their behavior back into appropriate limits, the teacher, without saying a word, hands them their test papers. Another example is Nate who always calls out answers. The teacher does not respond to Nate in any manner and, in fact, turns her back on the student, calling upon students who raise their hand. When Nate raises his hand, he immediately is called upon for the answer.

Several caveats must be given concerning the use of planned ignoring. Teachers obviously must not ignore behavior which is either physically or psychologically dangerous to any individual. Additionally, threats to property cannot be ignored. Behavior which is attracting the undue attention of other students also must not be ignored. If a decision is made to ignore a behavior, and then later the same behavior is attended to, the likelihood that planned ignoring will be effective in managing that behavior in the future is greatly reduced because of this inconsistency. Finally, with some students, such as those with ADHD, planned ignoring may be totally ineffective because often they don't notice that you are ignoring them.

When disruptive behavior is ignored, the behavior often initially intensifies, because the student is likely to conclude that a higher level of disruptive behavior is called for, in order for him to achieve his goal of distorted power. This leads many teachers to prematurely discontinue the strategy. However, if the student's behavior does not violate any of the above cautions, continued ignoring by the teacher often results in success. When teachers prematurely discontinue ignoring, it reinforces the student's increased level of disruptive behavior.

Signal Interference

When planned ignoring is either ineffective or not suitable under the circumstances, signal interference is the next intervention in the hierarchical scheme. Signal interference is the pre-planned and systematic use of body language or other signals that clearly communicates to the student that his behavior is inappropriate and/or communicates what is the desired appropriate behavior. Additionally, signals may communicate teacher approval of student behavior. Typical types of signal interference are facial expressions, eye contact, and hand gestures.

When a student is fooling around, often a look serves to signal the student that it's time to get back to work. If a student is roaming around the room, a finger pointed at his chair redirects him back to his desk. Another type of hand signal is the familiar finger to the lips to signal someone to stop talking. Simply shaking the head up and down or smiling indicates approval to the student.

The facial expression of the teacher must at all times be congruent with the message that the teacher intends to send to the student. Smiling while placing the finger to the lips in order to signal quiet is an example of an incongruent display and is liable to confound the message and confuse the student as to its meaning.

A strategy which oftentimes works well is to have mutually agreed upon signals which everyone in the class recognizes. For example when Ms. Allen stands at the doorway of the room, all her students recognize this position indicating it's time for recess, clear your desks, get your coats, and line up to go outside. When Ms. Chofnas flicks the lights, it is understood by the students to mean that it is too noisy and to talk more quietly. Ms. Aronow plays the C chord on the piano to communicate to her students to stop working at their learning centers and return to their desks. For students who are chronically disruptive, especially those with ADHD, private signals, mutually agreed upon, may not only improve on-task behavior but may increase the student's sense of significance and so improve the relationship between the teacher and the student. For example, a tug on the ear is agreed upon as the private signal to Harold that he needs to take out his book and begin work. This type of message frequently goes unnoticed by other students and is, in any case, meaningless to all but the targeted student.

A benefit of signal interference is that it can be utilized at a distance and therefore, as with planned ignoring, does not interfere with what the teacher and the rest of the class are doing. For example, the teacher may send a signal while continuing to work at the blackboard, from across the room, in the playground, or while running the overhead projector.

Proximity Interference

Students frequently behave more appropriately when the teacher stands near them. Therefore, teachers who move around the classroom prevent a good deal of misbehavior from occurring. If a discipline problem does occur, the teacher is in the position to rapidly move toward the student without everyone in the class being aware that a problem exists. However, if you typically do not circulate throughout your classroom, but then you move and stand next to a specific student who is off-task, you increase the confrontational nature of your proximity because it is a rare event. A relaxed teaching style in which you frequently walk around the room allows proximity to be a positive and encouraging condition as well as a signal to stop disruptive behavior. Whether proximity is encouragement or management depends upon the antecedent student behavior. If the student is on task, teacher proximity is probably encouraging in that it provides an opportunity for the student to display competence. If the student is off task, teacher proximity hopefully will be a reminder to return to task. Remember however, proximity control is a nonverbal intervention. Resist the urge to say something to the student about his behavior. Instead, conduct the class as usual, albeit from a different location.

Proximity control may be combined with signal interference to create an even more effective intervention. For example, if Ms. Nelson makes eye contact with Sam and then walks purposefully toward Sam's desk, it sends a stronger message to Sam.

Proximity control is more effective than planned ignoring or signal interference for the student with ADHD. These students are more likely to be aware of the location of the teacher than other nonverbal behavior that the teacher is exhibiting.

Touch

Touch is a highly effective but problematic intervention in today's classrooms. It used to be that teachers felt free to appropriately touch students. This is no longer the case. Although all people need to be touched, and most younger students seek touch, it is an intervention which must be very cautiously and very sensitively used. A touch on the shoulder or a hand on the shoulder or arm is an unmistakable signal. Whether that signal is positively or negatively perceived is a function of the student's past experiences with you and others, his particular sensitivity to touch, as well as a function of culture and the student's age. Some individuals are hypersensitive to touch either for reasons of physiological arousal, which is often true of students with ADHD, or a history of physical or sexual abuse, anxiety, or fear. Certain cultures encourage touch while others proscribe it. It is important, therefore, to know your student well before intervening with touch. If you frequently use touch to signal acceptance, approval, and affection, you increase the probability that touch as an intervention for disruptive behavior will not be resented because of this positive association. If, on the other hand, you touch students only as a way to manage disruptive behavior, the converse is true. As a general rule, younger students are more accepting of touch than are adolescents. Adolescents might frequently perceive touch as either aggressive or worse, sexual. If you doubt this, think of how often and at what age students seek to sit in your lap. To the kindergarten student of either gender, sitting in the teacher's lap during story time may be a real treat. However, certainly for an adolescent student to do the same would be highly inappropriate and likely would lead to serious allegations and/or sanctions against the teacher.

It is helpful when establishing class guidelines to spend a moment discussing all the ways in which you will intervene nonverbally, including the occasional use of touch; such an explanation further serves to avoid any negative responses. Having listed all of these concerns, nevertheless a slight touch to an off-task student effectively can alert the student and help him to choose more appropriate behavior.

When it is used, touch should be applied as light, non-aggressive, physical contact. It can be used to guide a student to appropriate conduct, such as when a teacher gently directs a student back to his seat. It also can serve to increase the efficacy of proximity control; for example, placing a hand lightly upon the shoulder of Joey whom the teacher is standing behind when Joey is throwing his pencil in the air and letting it hit the floor.

Although these nonverbal techniques have been presented in a hierarchical order, the sequential delivery represents an idealized classroom situation. In the real classroom, the sequence of delivery depends upon the characteristics of the individual student, the type of disruptive behavior, and the nature of the learning activity. For example, if a teacher observes Jeff firing spit balls at his neighbor, the teacher likely skips planned ignoring and signal interference in favor of proximity and removal of the straw.

It has been our experience that when teachers intervene with chronically disruptive students, they are less likely to use nonverbal techniques because the teacher has a low expectation of the students' ability to control themselves. We, however, believe that all students are capable of self-control. Therefore they should be given repeated opportunities to exert this control with nonverbal interventions before the teacher moves to verbal confrontation.

In a study conducted by Shrigley (1985), more than 50 teachers reported that 40 percent of all disruptive behavior was managed effectively using nonverbal interventions. In other words, close to half of all student disruptive behavior was managed without the teacher uttering a word or interrupting her lesson. The majority of the remaining disruptive behaviors are effectively managed by verbal intervention.

VERBAL INTERVENTIONS

After the application of various nonverbal techniques, what if the student is still disruptive? Many teachers now resort to threats, yelling, and punishment. These types of teacher behavior violate our five guidelines for effective intervention established at the beginning of this chapter. In addition, such negative interventions reduce the success/failure ratio, increase students' external locus of control, and foster students' distorted self-esteem. Contrast this to the following verbal interventions which represent the second tier of the hierarchy of intervention strategies. These verbal interventions continue to emphasize students' ability for self-control. They are less disruptive to the class than angry teacher displays. Although verbal interventions are more confrontational than nonverbal interventions, they are less likely to escalate students' disruptive conduct than are angry teacher displays. These verbal interventions continue to protect the physical and psychological safety of the student and preserve additional strategies for later teacher intervention.

We want to continue to signal students, now using verbal interventions, that their behavior is inappropriate and give them additional chances to choose appropriate behavior. While verbal interventions are somewhat confrontational, if done properly the confrontation is less likely to escalate. The suggestions below increase the possibility that students maintain an internal locus of control and reduce the movement toward distorted self-esteem.

→ Speak to the situation not the person (Ginott, 1972), or, as Albert Ellis (1975) says, "I am not a worm for behaving wormily." For example saying, "Gian, I do not like it when you yell at me," is vastly different than saying, "Gian, you are a very disrespectful person." Speaking to the person, as was done in the second statement, increases defensive and angry student behavior. It may very well lead to an increase in a distorted display of power.

→ Make the verbal behavior useable. Tell the student what you want him to do rather than point out what he is doing. "Ethan, I want you to raise your hand" rather than "Don't call out, Ethan."

→ Set limits on behavior, not feelings (Ginott, 1972). "Tyler, I can see you're angry, but you must keep your hands to yourself," not "Tyler, there's really no reason to be so angry."

→ Respect the student at all times. Limit the use of sarcasm and always avoid condescension.

→ Keep the interventions brief. This is not the time to dialog past and future events or to argue. Prolonged interventions take additional time away from instructional activities, and therefore they tend to be more disruptive. "Bruce, this is the third time today that I've had to speak to you about your behavior. Do you understand why you need to sit down? I've explained before that if I have to keep telling you to sit down, I will call your parents. Is that what you want me to do? Because I don't know any other way to get you to behave!" is less effective than, "Bruce, please sit down."

→ Keep the interventions as private as possible. The milder verbal interventions may generally be more public. However, as the level of confrontation rises, so does the need for privacy. You need to avoid providing a potential platform for the student to display distorted power.

→ Timeliness is very important. The further removed from the event your intervention is, the less impact it is likely to have. In contrast, the closer your intervention is to the event, the more impact it is likely to have.

Every verbal intervention is more confrontational than any nonverbal intervention. If you are at this point in the hierarchy, it necessarily must be because your use of nonverbal interventions has not been effective or the behavior is too serious to enter the hierarchy at the nonverbal level. Verbal interventions also are ordered, from those that are only slightly more confrontational than the nonverbal intervention of touch to increasingly more confrontational interventions. Verbal coping skills, in order of increasing confrontation include using a student's name, inferential statements, questions, I-statements, and demands.

Using a Student's Name

The first level of verbal intervention is using a student's name. Often, merely saying the student's name in the course of the lesson is effective in returning the student to on-task behavior. For example, Ms. M'fwumi says, "Netscape is a popular Internet browser, Joseph."

Another way to use a student's name is to call on the student. When using this method, it is less confrontational to say the student's name first and then ask the question. Asking the question first and then saying the student's name, as in "What were some of the events that led to the Berlin Wall being torn down, John?" virtually ensures the student will not answer correctly, because if he is not paying attention, then he has not even heard the question before his name is called. While this may be effective in regaining on-task behavior, it is more confrontational than needed, because it tends to embarrass the student in front of his peers.

Inferential Statements

Inferential statements are at the next level of verbal intervention. These statements serve to get the attention of the student in a good-natured way.

→ "Heidi, you seem to have a lot of energy today!" The teacher said this in order for Heidi to focus on her inappropriate wandering around the room and to increase the probability that Heidi will now sit down.

→ "Sommer, I'll bet you'll have a lot to talk to Sarah about at recess. The teacher made this statement to get Sommer to attend to the fact that she is talking to Sarah and to increase the probability that she will stop talking until recess time.

→ "Jerry, recess is only five minutes away." The teacher said this to increase the probability that Jerry will stay on task for another five minutes, because he knows that he will have a break in a few minutes.

It might appear to the reader that these interventions violate our guideline that verbal interventions need to tell students what we want them to do. At this point in the hierarchy, however, it is preferable to keep the level of confrontation low. A hint is often all that is needed to bring a student back to appropriate behavior. We have not yet reached the stage of directly telling the student what is expected. The teacher still is exhibiting significant respect for the student's ability to recognize what is expected of him and to choose more appropriate behavior without more teacher assistance.

Care must be taken when using inferential statements to avoid being overly sarcastic or snide. In the examples above, a subtle change in tone could have turned a mildly amusing comment, meant to get the student's attention, into a sarcastic comment which most certainly will be perceived as an attack on the student himself. If you respect your students and encourage a referent relationship, then you increase the probability that your inferential statements are perceived positively.

The use of adjacent reinforcers such as, "I like the way Carolyn and Andrea are sitting quietly," to get Steven sitting nearby back on task, is similar to inferential statements. However, it is the authors' opinion as well as Alfie Kohn's (1993), an authority on the difficulty with rewards and punishments, that adjacent reinforcers potentially tend to reduce the intrinsic motivation of Carolyn and Andrea by praising them, as discussed in Chapter 6. It also disrespects Carolyn and Andrea by using them to manipulate Steven. Adjacent reinforcement also does little to enhance their standing with the other members of the class by setting up a competition with Carolyn and Andrea in the lead. We therefore do not endorse the use of other students to remind or reinforce the behavior of their classmates.

Questions

Assuming the student is still disrupting the class, according to the hierarchy you next move to questions. Questions are designed to alert the student more directly to the inappropriate nature of his behavior. A question also alerts the student to the effect that his behavior is having upon other students in the class. The purpose of questions therefore is to help the student display pro-social virtue by altering his behavior in a manner that is not disruptive. Be mindful that these statements once again need to be delivered sincerely and without sarcasm or condescension, which reduces the possibility of the student in turn providing a sarcastic answer.

→ "Eddy, are you aware that tapping your pencil is disturbing the class?"
→ "Jesús, do you know that your humming makes it difficult for others to concentrate?"
→ "Tom, could you work a bit more quietly? The noise is distracting others!"

I-Statements

I-statements (Gordon, 1974) are slightly more confrontational and more directly communicate what behavior you desire of the student and why, as well as providing feedback about the effect of the behavior upon the teacher and the rest of the class.

I-statements are constructed using three components; they communicate 1) what the student is doing, 2) the effect the student's behavior has on the class, and 3) how the teacher feels about it. This is an example of assertive delivery, which is discussed in more detail in Chapter 8.

→ "Duc, when you tap your pencil it is difficult to concentrate on the math lesson. This disturbs me because I want everyone to do well in math."
→ "Jack, when you arrive late to class, it disrupts the lesson for everyone, and this bothers me because I want everyone to have enough time to learn the material."
→ "Ethan, when you pass notes to Thea it distracts both of you from your work, and this disturbs me because I would like you both to learn the lesson."

The use of I-statements, because they rely upon the student caring how the teacher feels about student behavior, is only effective if the teacher is perceived as a referent authority. If the student does not have this perception, disruptive behavior might actually increase after the use of I-messages as the student will now know which behaviors are likely to increase his distorted competence and power by making the teacher angry and otherwise feel upset.

Demands

At this point, all other methods having failed, the teacher makes a demand of the student. In general, demands are more effective when you tell students what you want them to do, rather than what you don't want them to do.

→ "Carey, return to your seat and continue working on problems 5 through 10," is more effective than "Carey, stop wandering around the class!"

→ "Aimee, put the paper away and start working on your computer journal," rather than "Aimee, stop writing notes to Pandit."

→ "Evan, put your coat in your cubby and begin answering the openers," not "Evan, don't put your coat on the floor!"

To the extent that you make the demands privately, you decrease the effect of "playing to the audience" and so you set up less of a power struggle between you and the student. Any struggle for power is, by definition, going to increase the student's distorted self-esteem. It is for this reason that for some students compliance is less of an issue if the entire class is not an audience for the demand. Again, be brief and to the point. This is not the time to reflect upon students' past transgressions or to editorialize upon the future. Comments such as, "This is the 5th time I've had to tell you! Don't you ever learn? Now SIT DOWN !" or "How do you expect to pass this class if you can't stay in your seat? SIT DOWN!" are not effective. The fact that a student has exhibited the same behavior previously is not of immediate importance in getting him to comply with this demand now.

The effectiveness of demands like I-statements is increased when they are delivered assertively. Demands should be made, with a firm but not loud voice, in close proximity to the student whenever possible, and with constant eye contact.

A Troubling Question

The use of verbal interventions are more confrontational and insistent than nonverbal interventions, particularly demands. Therefore the teacher runs the risk of communicating failure to the student, encouraging an external locus of control, and fostering distorted self-esteem. Because it is being made ever more explicit to the student that his behavior is inappropriate, this constitutes a failure experience. To the extent that the student believes he is being forced by the teacher to comply, the student perceives an external locus of control. To the extent that the student experiences failure and an external locus of control, he also experiences a decline in his sense of pro-social power and competence. To maintain a sense of self-esteem, the student is therefore likely to compensate for the deficits in pro-social power and competence by displays of distorted competence and power such as continued non-compliance, and/ or escalation of disruption.

At this point, the critical reader may ask, "Why would I ever use verbal interventions if I'm going to run the risk of increasing students' resistance and increasing their disruptive behavior?" The answer is that you have a responsibility to all students in your class to maintain an effective learning environment; so you must do something to stop this student's disruptive behavior and the nonverbal interventions have not worked.

How can you then minimize the negative impact of verbal interventions? You minimize possible negative consequences using verbal interventions by emphasizing the four factors of prevention, affective delivery, appropriate content, and separation of each incident.

First focus upon prevention. If you utilize the strategies outlined in Chapter 6 on effective instruction, facilitating intrinsic motivation, and encouraging pro-social self-esteem, then the student has an increased success/failure ratio, has moved toward an internal locus of control, and has experienced an increase in pro-social significance, competence, virtue, and power. Therefore, the student should be somewhat resistant to the potential negative effects of verbal interventions and the probability of success of verbal interventions is increased.

Secondly, focus on affective delivery. Throughout this chapter we have stressed that you must deliver verbal interventions assertively without anger, frustration, or condescension and do so in as private a manner as possible. This delivery increases the probability that the student will focus upon his behavior and not your behavior. Appropriate delivery encourages the student's development of an internal locus of control.

Thirdly, focus on the content of the verbal message. Communicate to the student your belief that the student always has a choice and is competent to make the appropriate choice, if given the opportunity. By modeling your interventions on the examples given for each verbal intervention, you communicate your belief that the student is competent and powerful. Thus, hopefully, the student uses his competence and power in a pro-social manner, and because of the possible positive impact upon the class, he also experiences pro-social virtue.

Lastly, it is crucial that each incident of disruptive behavior be treated as separate and discrete. When the student brings his behavior back into appropriate limits, he is welcomed back into the class community and is treated the same as every other student, as if nothing has happened. Obviously chronic student disruptive behavior may require additional intervention. These interventions are levels three and four of the hierarchy and are discussed in the next two chapters.

INTERVENING WITH STUDENTS WITH ADHD

Because students with ADHD are impulsive, teachers find themselves intervening more frequently. Furthermore, as explained previously, the nonverbal interventions are less likely to be effective with students with ADHD. Therefore teachers generally have to use more verbal interventions, particularly demands, and even more confrontational interventions, detailed in Chapters 8 and 9.

Students with ADHD also tend to have a lower success/failure ratio, have an external locus of control, and are extrinsically motivated and thus tend to find their self-esteem in more distorted ways. Because of their external locus of control, students with ADHD frequently wait to be told explicitly what to do before changing their behavior.

Due to these factors, teachers tend to rely less upon prevention and move rapidly through the hierarchy, giving brief if any attention to the non-verbals. Therefore these students are given less of an opportunity to experience the positive effects of controlling their own behavior. Since the teacher may be more frustrated with these students, she may deliver verbal interventions more aggressively. These teacher behaviors do little to increase the likelihood that students with ADHD develop a more positive success/failure ratio, intrinsic motivation, and pro-social self-esteem.

While students with ADHD do have a more difficult time developing self-control, they do eventually learn to bring their behavior into appropriate bounds, especially when signaled to do so. One of our main philosophies is that there is nothing vastly different in instruction and management that you need to do with disruptive students, including those with ADHD. You just have to do it better. Doing it better means adhering to the guidelines and suggestions discussed in this chapter and the following chapters and reflecting upon your behavior using the four focus areas addressed in the section "A Troubling Question." Additionally, doing it better means being even more aware of your negative emotional responses, such as frustration, so that you can continue to focus your positive attention on the student.

You may assume that all strategies and guidelines for intervention, those discussed already and those that will soon be discussed, apply to all children, including those with ADHD or any other disruptive behavioral disorder.

SUMMARY

This chapter begins the exploration of strategies to effectively manage discipline problems. The challenge for the teacher is how to intervene in a manner which preserves the positive growth students have experienced in their success/failure ratios, intrinsic motivation, and pro-social self-esteem and at the same time get them to cease their disruptive behavior. The concept of a hierarchical approach to intervention was introduced and shown to include a variety of teacher interventions. To assist teachers in deciding when and how to use these interventions so as to not erode the gains made by students in their success/failure ratios, intrinsic motivation, and self-esteem, five intervention guidelines were detailed. Teacher interventions should 1) provide the student maximum opportunity for controlling his behavior in appropriate ways, 2) be no more disruptive to the class than the student's behavior, 3) decrease the likelihood of a confrontation with the student, 4) protect the physical and psychological safety of the student, and 5) leave open the greatest number of opportunities for further intervention.

The first two levels of the intervention hierarchy, nonverbal and verbal interventions, were presented. The nonverbal interventions are planned ignoring, signal interference, proximity interference, and touch. The second level of the hierarchy is verbal interventions. These verbal interventions are using student's name, inferential statements, questions, I-statements, and demands. For each intervention, guidelines were listed for delivery which focus upon affective tone and content. The troubling question of "Why would I ever want to use verbal interventions if I'm going to increase student resistance and get more disruptive behavior?" was answered in terms of focusing upon the four areas of prevention, affective delivery, content delivery, and keeping the incident separate.

Finally it was stated that because students with ADHD are impulsive, teachers rely less upon prevention, intervene more frequently with them, deliver interventions more aggressively and move rapidly through the hierarchy. The negative effects of these behaviors were explained, and it was stressed that even though it may take students with ADHD more time for self-control, they should be given, just like all students, every opportunity to do so. By carefully following the guidelines and suggestions outlined in this and following chapters, teachers can effectively manage all students in their classrooms.

Concept Map

NONVERBAL AND VERBAL INTERVENTIONS

Least Confrontation

Provide Student with Maximum Opportunity for Controlling Behavior in Appropriate Ways

Not More Disruptive to the Class than the Student's Behavior

Decrease the Likelihood of Confrontation with Student

Protect the Physical and Psychological Safety of the Student, Class, and the Teacher

Leave Open the Greatest Number of Opportunities for Further Intervention

Most Confrontation

NONVERBAL

Planned Ignoring — only if →

Signal Interference

Proximity Interference

Touch — use sparingly due to →

Not Dangerous

Not Destroying Property

Not Attracting Undue Student Attention

Culture, Taken Aggressively, Age of Student, Sexual Implication

Speak to the Situation NOT to the Person

Tell Student "What to do," NOT "What not to do"

Set Limits on Behaviors NOT Feelings

Respect All Students

Brief

As Private as Possible

Deliver Close to Event

VERBAL

Using Student's Name

Inferential Statements

Questions

I–Statements

Demands

REFERENCES

Ellis, A., and Harper R. A., (1975). *A New Guide to Rational Living,* Hollywood, CA: Wilshire Book Co.

Ginott, H., (1972). *Between Teacher and Child.* New York: Peter H. Wyden.

Gordon, T. (1974). *Teacher Effectiveness Training.* New York: Peter H. Wyden.

Kohn, A. (1993). *Punished by Rewards.* Boston: Houghton Mifflin.

Levin, J. and Nolan, J. F. (1996). *Principles of Classroom Management: A Professional Decision-Making Model, second ed.* Boston: Allyn and Bacon.

Shrigley, R.L., (1985). Curbing student disruption in the classroom - Teachers need intervention skills. *National Association of Secondary School Principals Bulletin, 69, 7, 26-32.*

FREQUENTLY ASKED QUESTIONS

1. How much disruptive behavior should a teacher ignore in order to continue the lesson without losing control entirely?

2. When is it appropriate to skip the nonverbal interventions and move directly to verbal interventions?

3. If I know from past experience that a student responds only to demands, why should I waste my time with any other interventions?

4. You speak about communicating to the disruptive student that he has a choice as to whether or not to behave appropriately. If I can't get this student to comply, won't I lose authority with the rest of the class?

5. I teach very tough students. If I behave the way that you suggest, they will perceive me as being weak. How do I preserve the student's perception that I have power and they have to listen to me?

6. You talk about prevention being critical in the overall management plan. What about the first few weeks of class when there hasn't been time for preventative measures to be effective? Won't I need to be more confrontational?

7. How can you say that you're making a demand on a student when there's no mention of consequence for non-compliance?

Chapter 8

When Nonverbal and Verbal Interventions Aren't Enough: The Management of Disruptive Behavior by Applying Consequences

INTRODUCTION

This chapter describes the effective delivery of consequences as well as delineates the significant differences that exist between the use of consequences and punishments. It is hoped that by the end of this chapter you will understand that the use of consequences is a powerful technique that when delivered calmly and assertively, not only preserves students' pro-social self-esteem and intrinsic motivation, but also greatly increases the likelihood that students will choose to behave in more appropriate ways.

The last chapter outlined a management system which begins with teacher nonverbal behavior and moves to verbal behavior. However, once the teacher has gone through the nonverbal and verbal techniques and finally issues a demand for more appropriate behavior but the student continues to misbehave, the teacher then delivers consequences.

The delivery of consequences is near the bottom of the hierarchy and is thus a critical benchmark in the management of disruptive students. Putting it bluntly, you really want this technique to work, because if it doesn't, you have to use techniques (Chapter 9) which, although effective in curbing chronic behavioral problems, also require additional teacher time and effort and involve other professionals or parents.

CONSEQUENCES RATHER THAN PUNISHMENTS, NOT JUST A DIFFERENCE OF SEMANTICS

Punishment

The behaviorists' definition of punishment is any adverse consequence that decreases the occurrence of a targeted behavior. However, in the day-to-day classroom use, punishment means inflicting a painful experience on the student. The painful experience may be physical or psychological. Generally, physical punishments, such as spanking, shaking, pulling, or making a student stand for long periods of time, are recognized by most educators as being unethical and are thus rarely used today. When they are used, it is usually out of teacher frustration and anger or a lack of knowledge of viable alternatives.

Some teachers support their use of painful physical punishments with two commonly held beliefs (Clarizio, 1980). The first justification is that this method develops self-discipline, moral character, and responsibility. In reality, studies have correlated physical punishment with delinquency (Readers will recognize this as the display of distorted self-esteem.). The second justification is that physical punishment is the only form of discipline that some chronically disruptive students understand and to which they react. This has never been shown to be true.

Administrators eager to make effective changes in the way their schools or districts cope with chronic discipline problems should heed Dill (1995), who believes that a teacher's philosophy of discipline should be seriously considered when making decisions on hiring. He believes that teachers will be ineffective in carrying out progressive educational changes if they believe that students learn best when threatened, punished, prodded, or humiliated.

Educators and psychologists have reminded us continually of the limitations of physical punishment. Epstein (1979) stated, "There is no pedagogical justification for inflicting pain . . . .. It does not merit any serious discussion of pros and cons" (pp. 229 - 230). Clarizio (1980) stated, ". . . there is very little in the way to suggest the benefit of physical punishment in the schools, but there is a substantial body of research to suggest that this method can have undesirable long-term side effects" (p. 141). Even the very popular teacher-centered Assertive Discipline model warns that "Consequences should never be psychologically or physically harmful to the students . . . corporal punishment should never be administered" (Canter, 1989 p. 58).

There is also punishment which although non-physical produces psychological harm. Examples include screaming at a student, public reprimands, threats, and accusations. School work itself may be punishing as in extra assignments or writing 100 times "I will not . . .." Other examples of punishment are insulting comments or, as we have mentioned previously, speaking to the person rather than the behavior, such as "Lukesha, you really are a rude child," rather than "Lukesha, your calling out interferes and disturbs other students."

It is our belief that neither physical nor psychological punishment is effective in reducing inappropriate student behavior or increasing the likelihood of appropriate behavior. If it were, discipline problems in the schools would be a footnote in history and this book need not be written, because punishment has always been a dominant feature of most teachers' repertoire of management techniques.

When the goal of intervention is to enhance a student's ability for self-control, it is important that the student be able to focus on her behavior and its effects on herself and on others. Punishment clouds this self-focus by focusing the student's concern on the punisher the teacher and the punishment, rather than upon herself and her behaviors. The punishment is not perceived to be the result of the student's behavior; it is perceived to be the result of the teacher being mean, arbitrary, and hurtful. This leads to student rage, resentment, hostility, and a desire to get even with the teacher, "the one who did this to me." (Dreikurs, et al. 1982).

Punishment does not teach alternative acceptable behaviors. In fact, it models inappropriate behavior and reinforces a lower level of moral development, by teaching students that when they are older and in a position of authority, they can then punish others who might be younger or with less authority (Jones and Jones, 1981).

An often ignored, though in some cases a desired outcome of punishment, is making students feel bad about themselves. In addition, students view teachers as people who cause unpleasant things to happen. To avoid this negative self-concept and the person who facilitates it, students learn to avoid both the punishment and the punisher (Kohn, 1993).

This is accomplished through lying, cheating, or becoming better at not getting caught. Kamii (1991) delineated three possible outcomes of punishment: 1) calculation of risks, the spending of time trying to figure out how they can get away with something, 2) blind conformity, which fails to teach self-control, or 3) revolt, which may be put into action by additional disruptive behavior or by more covert means such as shutting down completely. The irony of punishment is that the more you use this distorted power to try and control others' behavior, the less real influence you have over them (Gordon, 1989). In other words, the more you try to control a person, the more necessary it is in the future to try to control them.

Because of the unintended outcomes of punishment (delineated by Kamii, above), teachers reason that even stricter punishment is needed. "After all, if I can hurt this kid badly enough, surely she'll behave eventually." Unfortunately, this vicious cycle does not lead to appropriate student behavior but instead to more disruption, aggression, and hostility (Kohn, 1993). Additionally, as students get older, they tend to become inured to punishment. As with rewards, the magnitude of punishment has to be increased while the probability of success decreases with age.

Consequences

So what's a teacher to do? Some readers may be thinking, "OK, I finally figured out that the authors think that kids should get away with anything. No matter what the behavior, we teachers have to be understanding, sensitive, and empathetic. After all, self-control is where it's at and let's not do anything that will teach this kid that there are other people in this world besides her." Yes, teachers want students to recognize that when they choose inappropriate behavior there is some concrete result. We also want this.

We believe students must be held accountable for their behavior. When students learn the cause and effect relationship that exists between how they choose to behave and the outcomes of their behavior, they experience an increase in power. Whether this power is expressed pro-socially or in a distorted manner is a function of whether the students focus on their own behavior or on the teacher's behavior. With the use of punishment, as stated above, the focus is on the teacher's behavior and his role as punisher. Students are therefore encouraged toward an external locus of control. The resultant feelings are likely to be insignificance, incompetence, and powerlessness. In order to make up for these deficits in self-esteem the student is very likely to express distorted significance, competence, and power.

So there needs to be a concrete result of student choice of inappropriate behavior, but that result must not be punishment. There are alternatives and they are natural or logical consequences.

Natural Consequences

Natural consequences are probably the most powerful learning experiences that we encounter and thus are significant modifiers of future behavior. Natural consequences have been described as the real world's classroom. Here are some common natural consequences.

→ Locking yourself out of the house because you misplaced your key.
→ Waking up on Sunday morning with a hangover because you drank too much Saturday night.
→ Having a car accident because you drove too fast.
→ Receiving painful sunburn because you sat in the sun too long.

All of these consequences have something in common. They are the result of action or inaction of the individual herself and do not involve the intervention of any other person. Thus, the only one responsible or "to blame" for the negative outcome is the individual who misplaced the key, drank too much, drove too fast, or sat in the sun too long.

Dreikurs (1964) emphasized that by allowing students to experience the natural consequences of their behavior, they are provided with an honest and real life learning situation. Primarily because of safety considerations, the use of natural consequences in a classroom is somewhat limited. For instance, the natural consequence of not following safety procedures in a science laboratory of an industrial arts class may be serious bodily harm. Nevertheless, whenever feasible and not dangerous, allowing students to experience the natural consequences of their behavior is a strong learning experience. Natural consequences clearly communicate the cause and effect relationship of behavioral choices and decrease the possibility of a negative inter-action between the teacher and student. Examples of natural consequences that students can experience in the classroom are:

→ Losing an assignment because of disorganization.
→ Having less time to complete a test because of coming to class late.
→ Falling and scraping one's knee due to running in the hallway.
→ Missing classwork due to cutting class.

Some teachers cannot resist the temptation to tell the student why the natural consequence occurred. For example, Mr. Blanco might say, "Gabriella, the reason you can't find your assignment is because you have such a sloppy notebook. I told you to get it organized or else this would happen." If you do this, you are in effect turning a valuable learning experience into a punishment. Gabriella obviously knows why the assignment is lost and doesn't need Mr. Blanco to tell her. By telling her, the focus switches to Mr. Blanco's behavior and is no longer on hers. So instead of the student thinking, "Man this is really a drag; I did that homework and I can't find it, and now I have to do it again;" the student is thinking, "What a moron Mr. Blanco is! What does he think I'm stupid or somethin?" When a natural conse-quence occurs, nature is the teacher, you do not have to do anything.

Logical Consequences

When natural consequences are not appropriate or do not occur, the teacher needs to intervene with a logical consequence. A logical consequence is a consequence which, although requiring the intervention of the teacher or another person, has some logical connection to the behavior which precedes it, and so it is not viewed as arbitrary or capricious. Like natural consequences, logical consequences are powerful influences on student behavior.

→ Mary needs to clean up the paint that she spilled on the floor during art.
→ Ellen is not called upon by the teacher, because she doesn't raise her hand.
→ Phylicia does not receive a copy of the test until she has her books put away.
→ Davida has to clean up the desk that she's written on.
→ Tamica has to stay after school to make up work that she missed by being late to class.
→ Francine has to work individually because she has not been cooperative with her group.
→ The principal calls the police because Alicia brought a knife to school.
→ Maya is pressing charges against Kristen because Kristen assaulted her in the lunchroom.

With the use of both logical and natural consequences, the focus is on the student behavior and its relationship to the consequence. The student is therefore encouraged toward an internal locus of control. The result is that significance and competence are not likely to be reduced, and power may actually increase in a pro-social manner. Therefore, there is no need for the student to express distorted significance, competence, or power. This is the reason that consequences as opposed to punishments 1) do not cause students to spend time trying to calculate risks in an effort to get away with misbehavior, 2) help students develop self-control and not just blindly conform, and 3) do not lead to additional disruptive behavior. In addition, consequences are effective at all age levels. Natural consequences tend to impact all individuals equally. Logical consequences are consistent with the cognitive development of students and their need for reasonable answers as to why things occur.

The following activity clearly illustrates the difference between the outcomes of consequences and punishments. Put yourself in the following situation. You are sixteen years old and have had your driver's license for less than a month. It's a Friday night and your parents have given you the new family car to drive for the evening. You pick up your friends and drive to the shopping mall. As you are pulling into a parking space, you cut the wheel too tightly and scrape the passenger side of the family car on the rear fender of a truck parked in the next spot. When you get out to examine the damage, there is a three-foot-long scratch along the side of your car. The truck has no damage. On arriving home later that night, you need to make a decision as to whether you will or will not tell your mother or father about the accident. You have three choices. Choice 1, don't say anything, and when the scratch is discovered in the morning, act surprised and claim that someone must have hit you when you were at the mall. Choice 2, tell your parent(s) that when you came out of the mall, you discovered that someone had hit the car and left no note. Choice 3, tell your parent(s) the truth. Think about how your parents would react and then decide how you would have broken the news.

This hypothetical situation has been proposed to hundreds of in-service and pre-service teachers with some interesting, but not unexpected, results. Those teachers who said they would lie by choosing options 1 or 2, relate that their parents would have screamed at them, grounded them, taken the car privileges away, or made them feel incompetent if they had told the truth. In other words, parents who usually punished generally would not have been told the truth. On the other hand, those teachers who said that they would have told the truth related that their parents would have required them to pay for the damages and/or required them to either take additional driving lessons or to go out with them so that they could learn to park the car better. Thus, parents who used consequences, rather than punishments, would be more likely to be told the truth. Those teachers that said they would choose options 1 or 2 would have learned to avoid punishment, but they would learn nothing about how to park a car without getting into an accident. Those who chose option 3 and took responsibility for their actions, learned the consequences of poor parking skill and were more likely to improve their parking skill in order to avoid negative consequences in the future. Additionally, they learned that they were responsible for "cleaning up their own mess" by paying for the damage to the car.

Table 8.1 summarizes the significant differences between natural and logical consequences and punishment.

TABLE 8.1 *Contrasting the Characteristics of Consequences and Punishment*

Natural and/or Logical Consequences	Punishment
naturally occurs or is logically related to student's behavior	does not naturally occur or is contrived
logical consequences are deliberately planned and delivered	usually is reactionary and arbitrary
illustrates cause and effect	illustrates the power of the teacher's authority
both are emotionally neutral, logical consequences are administered without anger	is emotionally charged, usually administered with anger
students focus on own behavior	students focus on the teacher as punisher
develops self-control	develops dependency on others
does not produce avoidance behaviors	produces avoidance behaviors
protects and/or builds self-esteem	erodes self-esteem
is congruent with moral development	is incongruent with moral development
effective for all age groups	becomes ineffective as students get older and punishments become less meaningful

The outcome of consequences is clearly more desirable to punishment. However, these outcomes are highly dependent upon the manner in which the teacher communicates and delivers consequences to the student.

THE DELIVERY OF CONSEQUENCES: "YOU HAVE A CHOICE"

At this point in the hierarchy, the teacher needs to make it clear to the student that her disruptive behavior must stop immediately or logical consequences will follow. There are two factors which determine the effectiveness of this intervention. First, there must be an explicit communication to the student that the teacher respects the student's right to choose how she is going to behave, even at this confrontational point in the hierarchy. Careful phrasing of the content of the message accomplishes this. The second factor is the delivery style or tone of the message. The teacher must remain fully in control of his affective expression so that the student takes the message seriously but without becoming defensive, which would change the focus of attention to the teacher's behavior rather than the student's own behavior.

Phrasing the Message

Loretta is disrupting the other students in her cooperative learning group in your classroom. You have moved through several nonverbal and verbal techniques without successfully influencing Loretta to change her behavior. You approach Loretta and say "Loretta, you have a choice. Work cooperatively with your team or move to the back of the room and work by yourself. You decide." Phrasing the delivery of consequences in this manner communicates to the student that the choice is hers to make and the outcome is dependent solely upon what she chooses.

If Loretta chooses to behave cooperatively, the disruptive behavior is something that happened in the past, and you treat her as if the disruption never occurred. However if Loretta continues to be disruptive, you again approach Loretta and say, "Loretta, you decided to move to the back of the room. Please move." Once Loretta has made her choice, the discussion is over. It is not appropriate to further penalize the student, for example with further negative comments or facial expressions just because she has not made the choice that you wanted her to make. The discussion is over, even if Loretta throws her chair backwards or uses profanity toward you on the way to the back of the room. We strongly suggest, due to the heightened tension of the moment, that unless Loretta is threatening the physical safety of her classmates or you, or destroying property, any discussion of the manner in which she has complied be deferred to a later time.

It is imperative that you not move to this level of the hierarchy unless you are ready to enforce the consequence. Preplanning is important because it is difficult to arrive at a logical consequence on the spur of the moment. The likelihood that you enforce the consequence is greatly increased if the consequence is a logical one.

Consequences determined in the heat of the moment are more likely to be harsh and less likely to be logically related to the disruptive behavior. For these reasons, spur of the moment consequences are more likely to be perceived as punishment, precisely what you are trying to avoid.

Delivering the Message

The manner in which you communicate, "You have a choice," is as important as its content in determining whether or not this technique is effective in influencing a student to change her behavior. Teachers increase the likelihood of the student choosing appropriate behavior by using an assertive response style. Assertiveness is often confused with aggressiveness. There is a fine behavioral line that distinguishes the two styles. When the teacher uses aggressiveness, the student is more likely to choose confrontation. In contrast, when the teacher uses assertiveness, the student is more likely to choose appropriate behavior.

Aggressiveness is a communication style in which the teacher clearly communicates what is expected but in a manner that abuses the right to choose and feelings of the student. This may be accomplished verbally or nonverbally. When teachers are aggressive, students often interpret the proposed consequences as threats of something that the teacher is going to do to them because the teacher is angry. This style reduces a students' sense of pro-social significance and power and may lead to an escalation of hostility and confrontation through the defensive display of distorted power. This display may be arguing with the teacher, refusing to comply with the consequence, and/or doing further disruptive acts.

An assertive response style is one in which the teacher also clearly communicates what is expected, but in a manner that respects the students' right to choose and students' feelings. In addition the teacher conveys that the student alone is responsible for the consequence of her behavior. When the teacher communicates this respect, the student feels no loss of pro-social significance. By communicating that the student is solely responsible for the outcome of her behavior, the student also is likely to feel an increase in pro-social power.

Assertiveness is a synergy of both nonverbal and verbal behavior. The message is delivered in as private a manner as possible; ideally only the teacher and student are present. In the classroom, however, the teacher should be in close proximity to the student without violating her personal space. The teacher maintains constant eye contact with the student while speaking in a firm, emotionally neutral voice, no louder than needed to allow the student to hear the message. The teacher's hands should be at his side, on the student's desk, or gently on the student's arm or shoulder. It is important to keep in mind the cautionary statements about touching students made in Chapter 7, most importantly that older students are likely to view touch when coupled with demands as aggressive or sexual.

Table 8.2 illustrates the differences between assertive and aggressive delivery styles.

TABLE 8.2 *Comparison Between Common Behaviors Associated with Assertive and Aggressive Styles of Communication of Consequences*

ASSERTIVE	AGGRESSIVE
usually private with student	often public in front of peers
in close proximity to student without violating personal space	often violates student's personal space
eye contact is made but face stays neutral	if eye contact is made, it is often with accompanying negative facial expressions, like frowning or narrowed eyes
voice is firm, neutral, soft	voice is often tense, loud, fast
hands at side, on students desks, or gently on student's arm or shoulder	hands on hips or folded at chest, or harshly touching the student
always uses student's name	often uses the pronoun "you"

THE STUDENT WON'T ACCEPT THE CONSEQUENCE; WHAT NOW?

You have delivered "you have a choice" assertively and Loretta continues to misbehave. Now you approach Loretta and say, "Loretta, you decided to move to the back of the room and work by yourself, please move." and Loretta says, "This is really unfair. I don't see you asking Michael to move and he's been talking all period." When this occurs, it is important that you do not get sidetracked, enter into a power struggle, or move to a more aggressive style. Instead, we suggest you remain assertive and use what Canter (1978) has called the "broken record" or "that's not the point" followed by another final "you have a choice."

Here is an illustration of how the integration of these techniques work.

Teacher (T): "Loretta, you have a choice. Begin working cooperatively with your group or move to the back of the room and work by yourself. You decide."

Loretta continues to be disruptive.

(T): "Loretta you have decided to move to the back of the room. Please move."

(L) "This is really unfair. I don't see you asking Michael to move and he's been talking all period."

(T): "Loretta, that's not the point. Please move to the back of the room."

(L): "You are always picking on me."

(T): "Loretta, that's not the point. Please move to the back of the room."

(L): "I might as well not even come to this class, I don't learn anything in here anyway."

(T): "Loretta, that's not the point. Please move to the back of the room."

(L): "I'm not going."

At this point, you should stop the broken record technique. Loretta is exhibiting a new disruptive behavior, and therefore it is time to point out to Loretta that she needs to make a different choice, or accept further consequences.

(T): "Loretta, you have a choice. Move to the back of the room, or I will ask Ms. Stehli (the aide or security person or vice-principal) to escort you to the office. You decide."

As illustrated, after two or three broken records, a final "you have a choice" is given. After this, the teacher disengages from the discussion with the student and follows through with the final consequence. Be careful not to threaten a consequence which you cannot or will not deliver. Instead, use a consequence with which you know you can and will follow through. Examples of some commonly used final consequences are removing the student from the classroom, contacting the student's parents to inform them of what occurred, or issuing a detention in order to discuss the matter further without taking more class time.

Just as you must keep in mind that a student is likely to feel insignificant and powerless when a teacher acts aggressively, and so the student may react with hostility and distorted displays of power; so too, you must be aware of your own feelings when a student behaves aggressively toward you. This student is trying to display distorted power by defying you and hopefully causing you to lose your temper, thus trying to change the focus away from her behavior and towards yours. It is therefore important that you remain calm and assertive. This is not a contest with a winner and a loser. You gain much more respect not only from the disruptive student, but from the rest of the students in your class, who are apt to be very interested at this point, if you remain in control of yourself, regardless of whether or not the student complies.

SUMMARY

This chapter described consequences and their purpose in managing disruptive behavior. First, the significant differences between punishments and natural and logical consequences were described. Punishments were shown to deprive students of the opportunity to learn appropriate behavior, because they are not logically related to the misbehavior, do not teach acceptable alternative behavior and model inappropriate behavior. In addition, punishment deprives a student of pro-social power and competence, thereby increasing the probability that the student will display distorted power with further disruptive behavior.

Consequences teach students appropriate behavior and are logically connected to their misbehavior. They do not effect negatively student pro-social power or competence. Therefore they do not increase the possibility of further disruptive behavior.

There are two types of consequences, natural and logical. Natural consequences do not require the intervention of another person whereas logical consequences do. The delivery of consequences was explained through the use of the technique, "You have a choice." It was stressed that both the phrasing of the message and delivery style were important factors in the effective use of this technique. Guidelines were provided for both the verbal and nonverbal behaviors of the teacher in implementing the technique. Emphasis was placed on delivering the consequences assertively rather than aggressively.

The "broken record" was introduced as a technique to be used when the student refuses to accept the consequences of her choice. The need for the teacher to remain in control and assertive at all times during his confrontation with the student was continually stressed.

Concept Map

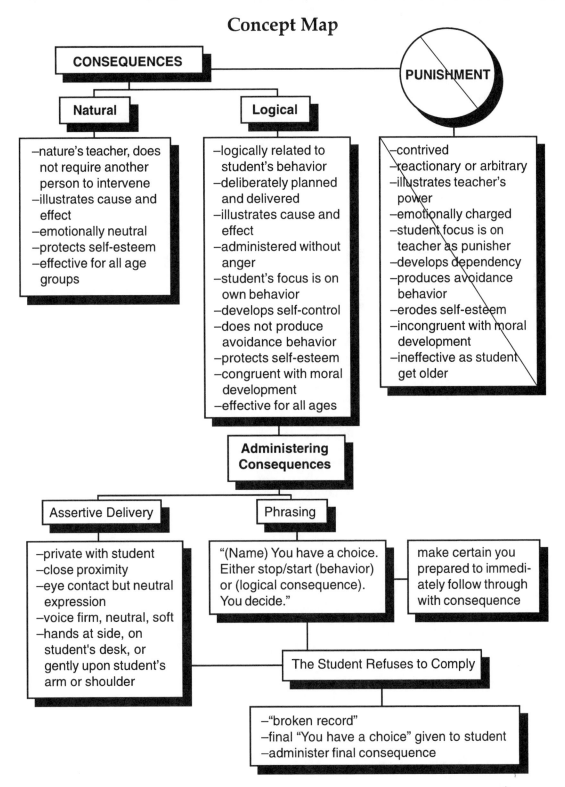

CONSEQUENCES

PUNISHMENT

Natural

–nature's teacher, does not require another person to intervene
–illustrates cause and effect
–emotionally neutral
–protects self-esteem
–effective for all age groups

Logical

–logically related to student's behavior
–deliberately planned and delivered
–illustrates cause and effect
–administered without anger
–student's focus is on own behavior
–develops self-control
–does not produce avoidance behavior
–protects self-esteem
–congruent with moral development
–effective for all ages

–contrived
–reactionary or arbitrary
–illustrates teacher's power
–emotionally charged
–student focus is on teacher as punisher
–develops dependency
–produces avoidance behavior
–erodes self-esteem
–incongruent with moral development
–ineffective as student get older

Administering Consequences

Assertive Delivery

–private with student
–close proximity
–eye contact but neutral expression
–voice firm, neutral, soft
–hands at side, on student's desk, or gently upon student's arm or shoulder

Phrasing

"(Name) You have a choice. Either stop/start (behavior) or (logical consequence). You decide."

make certain you prepared to immediately follow through with consequence

The Student Refuses to Comply

–"broken record"
–final "You have a choice" given to student
–administer final consequence

REFERENCES

Canter, L. (1989). Assertive discipline—More than names on the board and marbles in a jar. *Phi Delta Kappan, 71,* 1, 57-61.

Canter, L. (1978). *Assertive Discipline.* Belmont, CA: Wadsworth.

Clarizio, H. F. (1980). *Toward Positive Classroom Discipline,* 3rd ed. New York, NY: Wiley.

Dreikurs, R. (1964). *Children and the Challenge.* New York, NY: Hawthorne.

Dreikurs, R., Grundwald, B. B., and Pepper, F. C. (1982). *Maintaining Sanity in the Classroom, Classroom Management Techniques,* 2nd ed. New York, NY: Harper and Row.

Dill, V. (1995). Editorial: Why Care About Selection? Excerpt from The Haberman Newsletter. 1, 2.

Epstein, C. (1979). *Classroom Management and Teaching: Persistent Problems and Rational Solutions.* Reston, VA: Reston Publishing Co.

Gordon, T. (1989). *Teaching Children Self-Discipline . . . at Home and at School.* New York, NY: Times Books.

Jones, V. F., and Jones, L.S. (1981). *Responsible Classroom Discipline: Creating Positive Classroom Learning Environments and Solving Problems.* Boston: Allyn Bacon.

Kamii, C. (1991). Toward autonomy: The importance of critical thinking and choice making. *School Psychology Review, 20,* 382-88.

Kohn, A. (1993). *Punished by Rewards.* New York: Houghton Mifflin

Shrigley R. L.(1985). Curbing student disruption in the classroom—Teachers need intervention skills. *National Association of Secondary School Principals Bulletin, 69,* 479, 26-32.

FREQUENTLY ASKED QUESTIONS

1. How does a teacher determine what are logical consequences?

2. Aren't there some disruptive behaviors that have no logical consequences? How does a teacher deal with these behaviors?

3. How many times should I administer the same consequence to a chronically disruptive student? Doesn't the consequence have to get more severe?

4. I have a student in my class who keeps accepting the consequence when I use "You have a choice." What should I do now?

5. If I do as you suggest and use "You have a choice," won't I just have a classroom full of students who choose to do anything they want?

6. You say that it is important to maintain eye contact with the student. What if they look away?

7. You say to basically ignore the way a student complies with a consequence. If I have a student walking to the back of the room cursing and who maybe throws her chair, and I don't do anything, what will the rest of the students think?

Chapter 9

Managing the Remaining Behavior Problems: The Chronically Disruptive Student

INTRODUCTION

Ashley is still disrupting your class, despite your nonverbal and verbal interventions and the delivery of consequences via "You have a choice." It is at this point that many teachers seriously consider leaving the profession and opening a fruit juice bar in the mall. Short of this type of drastic solution, what remains that you can do to increase the likelihood that Ashley brings her behavior into appropriate bounds?

In this chapter we explore various techniques which increase teacher confidence to handle even the most chronically disruptive student who may be found in a regular classroom. These are the most confrontational techniques at the last level of the hierarchy, but they are still designed to protect the student's success/failure ratio, intrinsic motivation, and pro-social self-esteem. Just as in the whole hierarchy, and within each of the three levels already discussed, the techniques within this fourth and final level of the hierarchy are grouped from the least to the most confrontation.

"BAD KIDS"

The temptation at this point is to think that if you have not been successful so far, you must be dealing with inherently "bad kids." Recalling the discussion on avoiding labeling in Chapter 3, if you take this *bad kids* view, you will be more inclined to be harsh and punitive in your approach, further alienating an already distant and discouraged student. In addition, your negative interactions will reduce students' success/failure ratio. By being punitive you encourage the student to develop an external locus of control thereby fostering extrinsic motivation. By using distorted power to protect your own self-esteem, you necessarily encourage students' use of distorted power to protect their own self-esteem.

When working with very disruptive students, successful teachers must restructure their thoughts about these students in order to foster positive feelings which are essential for positive actions (Brendtro et al., 1990). If you continue to have positive expectations for Ashley and focus upon her behavior, not on her moral fiber, and if you continue to have confidence in your own instructional and management efficacy, then you send a message to Ashley that is positive and hopeful. This message very well may be, "I still believe that you have the ability to control your behavior in appropriate ways, and I am willing to give you the opportunity and support to do so."

The most effective action teachers can take at this point is to write on a large Post-it Note, "The only one I can control is myself." Place this note on your desk, in your roll book, or any other place where you frequently look. Refer to this note often. By encouraging you to focus upon your own behavior, you may find that this reminder helps to renew your strength and confidence to continue with the difficult task that lies ahead, helping this student gain the self-control needed for appropriate behavior. Successfully intervening with these very difficult students and building positive relations with them is an "endurance event" (Brendtro, et al., 1990, p. 65).

PREPARING TO INTERVENE WITH THE CHRONICALLY DISRUPTIVE STUDENT

Before deciding upon further interventions, take a step back and assess what has occurred up to this point. This will enable you to continue to make professional, pre-planned decisions and not be reactive or make it up as you go along. This assessment also provides feedback which may encourage you to retrace your steps and return to earlier levels of the hierarchy where appropriate. We suggest the use of two interrelated techniques, keeping anecdotal records of both student and teacher behavior and using anecdotal records to develop the Teacher Individual Management Action Plan.

Anecdotal Record Keeping

Anecdotal records (Levin and Nolan, 1996) provide both the needed data for teachers to intervene effectively with a chronically disruptive student and the justification for those interventions. The appropriate time to start an anecdotal record is actually before it is necessary to use the techniques for chronic behavior problems discussed in this chapter. We suggest that when a teacher is working with a student who repeatedly is disruptive and is requiring frequent nonverbal and verbal interventions, she start an anecdotal record. If the student brings her behavior into appropriate limits the anecdotal record can be saved in case the problem surfaces again in the future. If the student chooses not to control her behavior in appropriate ways, the record serves as data to support the teacher's use of her best professional practice. Additionally, it serves to justify future interventions and is invaluable as a means to accurately communicate to either her parents or other professionals what the student's behavior has been and what subsequent interventions you have used.

An anecdotal record is a brief, succinct account of observed student behavior and teacher interventions. This includes both appropriate and disruptive student behavior as well as what the teacher has done to encourage the student and manage the inappropriate behavior. Initially this record is only for the teacher's use. The student does not need to know that it is being kept. Many formats serve the purpose. From our experience, a pre-printed form, easily produced with any word processing software, works very well. Figure 9.1 illustrates a suggested format and the type of observations that need to be recorded.

| Student Name: <u>Ashley</u> | | |
| Phone Number:_____ | | |

DATE	STUDENT BEHAVIOR and RESPONSE TO INTERVENTION	TEACHER ACTION
2/19	1. Ashley arrived late to class	1. said nothing to her, will talk with her after class
	2. began to participate in class	2. called on her frequently, used her answers to continue lesson
	3. called out that Lee's answer was stupid	3. made eye contact with her
	4. passed notes to Valerie and refused to work with Taylor	4. used proximity control
		5. spoke with her after class about lateness, she said she will make it on time from now on

FIGURE 9.1 *Sample Anecdotal Record Format*

If the student does not begin to exhibit more appropriate behavior even though the teacher has intervened nonverbally, verbally, and delivered logical consequences, it is necessary to make decisions concerning the use of techniques for managing her chronically disruptive behavior by completing the Teacher Individual Management Action Plan (TIMAP). The data that has been collected in the anecdotal record is used to complete the TIMAP.

Teacher Individual Management Action Plan

A TIMAP is the teacher's analysis of the student's behavior and the teacher's interventions and is a necessary prerequisite before deciding which intervention the teacher will use next. The TIMAP is designed to: 1) objectively describe the student's behavior, and why it is a discipline problem, 2) examine what the teacher has done to encourage the student toward appropriate self-control, 3) analyze the verbal and non-verbal interventions used, 4) determine the natural and logical consequences of student behavior, and whether or not they were allowed to occur, and 5) plan for future interventions. Figure 9.2 is an example of a TIMAP and the questions the teacher needs to answer.

Student's Name ____Ashley_____

1. **Specifically describe the student's behavior.**

    It is important here to be concrete and specific. Global statements such as "Ashley annoys the other students," are not as effective for planning purposes as "Ashley repeatedly hits other students when she gets angry." The information in the anecdotal records that have been kept can serve to answer this question.

2. **Why is this problem a discipline problem?**

    As we have stated, not all problem behaviors are discipline problems. An objective evaluation by you of the student's behavior helps determine if you are reacting to observed, nondisruptive, although annoying, behaviors such as daydreaming, unpreparedness, or wearing a hat, as if they were discipline problems. If the teacher determines that the problem behaviors are not in fact discipline problems (see Chapter 1), then when answering questions concerning interventions, the teacher must carefully analyze the interventions that she lists for their appropriateness. Jamie, a student who daydreams because she is not interested in the content of the geography lessons, will not be brought back on task using techniques intended to manage chronic disruptive behavior.

3. **What techniques have you employed to prevent disruptive behavior?**

    Review Chapters 4, 5, and 6 and examine how your interventions have impacted the student's success/failure ratio, her intrinsic motivation and her prosocial self-esteem.

4. **What nonverbal and verbal interventions have you used thus far to help manage this student's behavior?**

    Referring to Chapters 7 and 8, specifically analyze the verbal and nonverbal interventions that you have used with the student. Refer once again to the anecdotal record to answer this question. Did you move too rapidly through the intervention hierarchy? Did you skip any interventions that might now be useful to try? Did you deliver the interventions in a referent manner?

5. **What are the natural and logical consequences of the student's behavior and did they occur?**

    Did you allow the natural consequences of the student's behavior to happen or did you intervene to prevent their occurrence? If logical consequences were promised, were they delivered appropriately, using "You have a choice?"

6. **What techniques are you now going to employ to manage this student's chronic behavior problem?**

    You will have to familiarize yourself with the techniques presented later in this chapter to complete this answer.

FIGURE 9.2 *Development of a Teacher Individual Management Action Plan*

Studying the TIMAP, the teacher asks herself a few questions. Is this student's behavior really a discipline problem, or is it another type of problem that is better managed by techniques other than those intended for discipline problems? Did I really attempt to encourage the student? Did I effectively employ both nonverbal and verbal interventions, or did I make rapid jumps through the hierarchy? If appropriate, did I let natural consequences occur? Did I assertively deliver logical consequences? If the teacher has doubts about any of her answers to these questions, she may want to consider going back to earlier techniques before using those intended for students with chronic behavior problems. If on the other hand, the teacher is satisfied with her interactions with the student, she is now ready to implement techniques from the last level of the hierarchy intended for chronic behavior problems.

A HIERARCHY FOR CHRONIC BEHAVIOR PROBLEMS

You already have given Ashley many opportunities to control her behavior. At this point, many teachers feel that their only alternative is to remove Ashley from the class. Although this might ultimately be necessary, there are several additional, highly effective techniques that you can use to encourage Ashley's compliance. If removal from the class becomes necessary, the anecdotal record, which is still being kept, the TIMAP, and the fact that you have employed one or more of the techniques in this chapter is more than enough support for this intervention. More importantly, however, they serve as valuable data for any other professional who may need to be consulted.

Many teachers ask how fast they should move through the techniques for chronic behavior problems and how many techniques should they employ? Although there is no hard and fast rule and it is best to use professional judgment based upon the individual student, we offer some guidance. The movement through this level of the hierarchy is a function of the degree of the disruptiveness of the student's behavior and efforts made by the student towards self-control. If you observe what appears to be genuine effort for appropriate self-control, then you may allow more time for success for any one technique or you may be more willing to intervene with additional techniques. However, if the student is "blowing you off", or if she is not expending reasonable effort to curtail her disruptive behavior, then you rapidly shift to another strategy and limit the number of interventions. When the behavior is not very disruptive, you may allow more time for success or try additional interventions, even in the face of low effort. If on the other hand, the behavior is very disruptive or dangerous, you may decide to go directly to the interventions at the end of the hierarchical structure. The speed of movement and the number of techniques to employ is illustrated in Table 9.1.

TABLE 9.1 *Speed of Movement Through and Number of Techniques to Use in the Hierarchy*

	NOT VERY DISRUPTIVE BEHAVIOR	VERY DISRUPTIVE BEHAVIOR
HIGH STUDENT EFFORT TOWARDS SELF-CONTROL	slow movement through hierarchy, many techniques	moderate movement through hierarchy, moderate number of techniques
LOW STUDENT EFFORT TOWARDS SELF-CONTROL	moderate movement through hierarchy, moderate number of techniques	rapid movement through hierarchy, few techniques

Interventions for chronic behavior problems follow the same guidelines as for non-chronic behavior problems: maximize opportunities for student self-control, be no more disruptive to the class than the student's behavior, decrease the likelihood of a confrontation with the student, protect the physical and psychological safety of all students, and leave open opportunities for further intervention.

There are eight interventions for managing chronic behavioral problems and are ordered from the least to the most confrontational. These are 1) teacher/student conference, 2) student self-monitoring, 3) student problem solving, 4) contracting for change, 5) anecdotal record keeping with student participation, 6) conditional removal of the student from class, 7) parent/teacher conference, and 8) referral to outside professionals.

Keep in mind, with each step in the hierarchy the teacher's work load increases, the student has fewer future choices and opportunities to demonstrate self-control, and the possibility of the teacher and student developing anger and resentment towards each other is heightened. To minimize the concern of student anger and resentment, the teacher has shown and continues to show respect and positive regard for the student and has endeavored to gain her trust in the teacher as a reliable, caring adult. Remember we are not suggesting that a teacher employ each and every technique.

Teacher/Student Conference

The authors have repeatedly stated our belief that effective teachers always attempt to establish caring, respectful relationships with all of their students. Therefore, conferences are not limited to only those times when the teachers and a student have a problem. We do not want students to view meeting with the teacher as an aversive condition. Thus it is important to meet frequently and privately with students to discuss positive events and not only negative ones.

The meeting now taking place, however, is to discuss the student's continued, disruptive behavior. In this conference you assertively tell the student what you've observed, how you feel about it, and what you want the student to do. You also ask the student what her perception is, how you can assist her, and inquire as to why she feels the problem is persisting. You do not argue with the student. You have the anecdotal records. You know what you've observed, and now the question becomes "what is the student going to do to rectify the situation?"

Showing the student the anecdotal record of her behavior tells her not only what specific disruptive behaviors have been observed but that you have gone to considerable effort to document the difficulties that she is having. It also tells her what success she has experienced and how you have tried to help. She is now aware of the seriousness with which you view the problem. She is also aware that you care enough about her to take the time to document her classroom behavior, both positive and negative. Whether or not this is perceived positively or negatively by the student is in large part a function of your respectful interactions with the student up to this point and the continued respect that you show her during the conference. Keep in mind the previously mentioned principle which emphasizes not attacking the person of the student, but focusing upon observed behavior instead. Make certain to point out the positive notations in your record not just the negative. There should be no doubt of your resolve to protect the learning environment of your class, regardless of the decisions she may make about her own conduct. She needs to come away from the conference knowing that while you will help and encourage her, you will not tolerate her continuing to make choices which create a discipline problem. This is an opportunity for the student to make a commitment to you and to herself to change her behavior. The meeting, whether or not she makes a commitment for change, and her behavior during the conference is recorded in front of the student on the anecdotal record.

Student Self-Monitoring

If the teacher/student conference does not result in a positive change in the student's behavior, self-monitoring is initiated. Self-monitoring techniques are very effective for the student who wants to behave more appropriately but seems to need frequent reminders to do so. It is a way for the student to take control of her behavior by giving herself these reminders. To make it easier for the student to learn how to self-monitor and to increase the probability of initial student success, it is important that the self-monitoring instrument focus on only one or a very few behaviors to start.

The manner in which this technique is explained to the student significantly influences the likelihood of success or failure. If it is viewed as a punishment, the technique takes on all the drawbacks associated with punishments and the likelihood of success is diminished. On the other hand, if it is viewed as a way for the student to help herself with teacher support and encouragement, there is a greater likelihood of the student improving her behavior.

To be effective, the student must understand clearly how to use the instrument and the specific behaviors that are being monitored. When students first begin using self-monitoring, some may need cues from the teacher as to when to check their behavior. The more private the cue, the better. Private cues actually communicate pro-social significance to the student. As the student learns to self-monitor, the need for teacher cues will diminish.

Self-monitoring also may take place in tandem with teacher monitoring, where the mutually agreed upon target behavior is monitored by both the teacher and student. At the end of a specified period of time, the student and teacher compare records. The goal here is to not only increase the student's appropriate behavior, but to help the student to be more accurate in self-appraisals.

The teacher must keep in mind, when using this technique or any other designed to help change chronic disruptive behavior, that she is attempting to modify long term, and possibly habitual, negative behavior. Success may come in small steps with frequent lapses in progress. These behaviors did not develop in a day, and they will not be replaced by new appropriate behaviors in a day. The teacher must remain patient. In the beginning, focus on the effort that the student is making to change her behavior rather than the actual behavioral change.

A very simple method of self-monitoring is to have the student place a sheet of paper on a section of her desk with a grid, in which the student monitors and records every occurrence of her appropriate and inappropriate behavior, as shown in Figure 9.3. The student simply puts a check mark in the corresponding box every time she displays an appropriate behavior and every time she displays an inappropriate behavior. It does not matter which box the student checks. If her behavior is appropriate, fine. If her behavior is inappropriate, then her check is a signal to her to change her behavior. Of course the teacher must be sure that the student clearly understands what behaviors are being monitored. For Ashley's first self-monitoring task, inappropriate behavior was defined as making fun of other students' answers. Appropriate behavior was not making fun of other students' answers. If the initial self-monitoring is successful, then Ashley and her teacher can design another instrument to self-monitor additional behavior.

I did NOT make fun of another student's answer	I MADE fun of another student's answer

FIGURE 9.3 *A Simple Self-Monitoring Instrument (Occurrence Schedule)*

Another type of self-monitoring instrument is one that is on a time interval schedule. For example, the student monitors her behavior every 15 minutes, as illustrated in Figure 9.4. This type of instrument is appropriate for helping students stay on-task during seat work or direct teacher instruction.

TIME	Am I ON Task?	Am I OFF Task?
8:00		
8:15		
8:30		
8:45		
9:00		
etc.. . .		

FIGURE 9.4 *A Simple Self-Monitoring Instrument (Interval Schedule)*

Self-monitoring, if handled effectively, increases a student's sense of pro-social competence and power, as the student sees herself making positive progress. This also serves to encourage an internal locus of control. If the student has agreed to participate and has set her own goals, achievement of those goals is the only positive consequence needed.

Student Problem Solving

If the self-monitoring is not successful, the teacher schedules another teacher/student conference. At this conference, the student again is informed that her behavior is interfering not only with her own learning, but also with the right of her classmates to learn. At this conference however, just a commitment of improved behavior is not enough. The student is now asked to brainstorm several different strategies to decrease the occurrence of disruptive behavior. Any suggested strategy, no matter how bizarre or unlikely to result in appropriate behavior is written down and discussed. This serves the dual purpose of respecting the student's point of view and problem solving capabilities and also provides some levity, if some really bizarre solutions are considered. It will be tempting for you to pre-determine what the successful strategy is and to attempt to sway or manipulate the student into accepting your solution. It is our opinion that students who devise their own strategies or who feel empowered to choose among several strategies are more likely to adhere to the strategy after the meeting.

A suggested format to assist the student in problem solving involves a pre-printed sheet of questions which the student answers in writing. The questions with Ashley's answers follow.

1. **What is the problem?**
    I keep making fun of Lee's answers.
2. **What can I do about it?**
    I can put tape over my mouth. I can not say anything at all in class. I can write myself a big note that says, "Don't make fun!"
3. **What is the best solution?**
    I'll write myself a note and tape it to my desk.
4. **I agree to follow the solution.**

    Student signature _____

When a number of strategies are listed, the student and the teacher try and agree upon one or two likely solutions. During the discussion the more bizarre or unlikely to succeed strategies are evaluated and discarded. For example, the suggestion of another opportunity to self-monitor disruptive behavior is rejected because it has previously failed to result in more appropriate behavior. However, self-monitoring may be used to assess the progress of other strategies that result from this conference. Elementary students will obviously need more assistance with problem solving than older students.

When the meeting is finished, the student has a clear action plan which she agrees to put effort into implementing. If the student refuses to agree to a solution, the teacher moves to other interventions in the hierarchy. The meeting with the student and the student's behavior during the conference is noted in her anecdotal record in front of the student. After the student sees you do this, she is given the opportunity to check the accuracy of what you have written.

This strategy is designed to develop the student's internal locus of control and thus intrinsic motivation. In addition, when this conference is appropriately conducted with respect toward the student, the teacher increases the probability that the student's pro-social significance and competence are enhanced.

Contracting for Change

If student problem solving is ineffective in encouraging appropriate student behavior, a more formal intervention is called for. Contracting for change is designed to further impress upon the student what is expected of her and to receive from the student a concrete promise of positive behavioral change. A contract is a document which is mutually developed and agreed upon. Writing out your demands and getting a student to sign off on them by promising a reward or punishment is not a contract; it is extortion and has all the drawbacks associated with punishment. Even now, we must recognize the student might not agree to a contract, or there may not be legitimate student desire to bring her behavior into appropriate limits. In these cases the teacher may decide to forgo the contract and proceed to techniques further along in the hierarchy.

A conference to develop a student contract begins by outlining your observations and assessing the student's understanding of the seriousness of the situation. In addition the need for a contract as a method to help the student make positive changes is thoroughly explained. The student is told what she needs to accomplish and is then asked what changes she will make in her behavior. While the terms of the contract are negotiable, the need for the student to change to more appropriate behavior is not. If you feel the student is being vague, is unrealistic, or is setting up roadblocks, don't sign off on the contract; instead consider moving to a different technique.

Each contract's specifics are necessarily different. However each contract generally should include 1) the behavioral goal(s), 2) the strategies to reach the goal(s), 3) a method for determining whether the goal(s) has been met, 4) an agreed upon time to meet and discuss the student's progress, and 5) a place for both teacher and student signatures.

After having discussed and specified the conditions of the contract, both you and the student sign and date the agreement. The private conference and the student's behavior during the conference is recorded on the student's anecdotal record, and the student is again asked to attest to the accuracy of what is recorded.

Sometimes contracts do not result in student behavioral change. This is usually a result of one or a combination of three factors. The first is that the statement of the goal(s) is unclear to the student or the teacher, or there are too many goals stated. Therefore, student goals need to be few and clearly specified so that there are no student or teacher misunderstandings as to what is expected. Secondly, because this student has a history of disruptive behavior, there is a tendency on the part of the teacher to expect the student to correct the problem once and for all! This is highly unrealistic and sets up a situation that is more likely to result in failure than success. Problems that have existed for long periods of time do not just disappear because a contract has been written. Write goals which are successive approximations of the appropriate behavior. In other words, these goals can be successfully met without students having to undergo a total behavioral change all at once. Once these goals are met, the student feels some success and is now ready to set additional goals in a series of successive contracts. Thirdly, many contracts result in less than desirable outcomes, because the time period between teacher and student progress checks is too long. In the beginning of the contract, progress checks might occur five or six times a day for elementary school students and twice a week for older students. As the student's behavior begins to change, the time between progress checks is lengthened. Figure 9.5 shows a well designed contract for an elementary school student.

Name: <u>Ashley</u>

1. Expected Behavior
    Ashley will not make fun of other students during reading time.

2. Time Period
    The week of 2/19 to 2/23.

3. Evaluation
    Self-monitoring instrument and teacher monitoring.

4. Progress checks
    Each day after reading time and before recess.
    A meeting with Ms. Allen on Friday 2/23 at 2:50 PM to discuss the week's progress and talk about next week's contract.

Student Signature: _____ Date: _____
Teacher Signature: _____ Date: _____

FIGURE 9.5 *Sample Contract*

Some teachers may look at the sample contract and think there is no place to specify what the rewards are for improved student behavior. For reasons that have been detailed in Chapter 6, we believe that it is not appropriate to promise the student a reward or to threaten the student with a punishment for compliance or non-compliance. The student complies with the contract, because it is her desire to accomplish the goals she has outlined, not because of some extrinsic reward. However, for some students you may decide that it is necessary to provide some incentives for improved behavior. Although we are, in general, opposed to this, if you decide to offer incentives, we suggest that they be directly related to learning such as additional computer time, working with special educational computer games, or learning more about computers and not the tangible rewards of candy, smiley faces, or tokens to be cashed in later for special prizes or privileges. There are, of course, consequences for repeated refusal to cease disruptive behavior. However, it is not appropriate to hold those consequences up to the student as the next step, mainly because to threaten the student tends to decrease compliance and fosters an external locus of control.

Once the contract has begun, carefully monitor and record the student's progress in attaining her goals in her anecdotal record. This record provides accurate data to discuss at your next conference with the student.

Anecdotal Record Keeping with Student Participation

When the student fails to participate in one of the previous techniques or continues to be a discipline problem in the classroom, there is one technique left before the student must leave the classroom. This is to have the student become an active participant in the use of anecdotal records. The student is already aware that the teacher has been recording her daily behaviors, both appropriate and disruptive, and has seen the teacher make notations in the record after each teacher/student conference. Now the student is made aware of what the teacher is recording daily.

A private conference is again scheduled with Ashley. She is shown the anecdotal record and is informed that at the end of the morning and at the end of day she will be required to read what you have written and sign the record (for secondary students the reading and the signing of the record takes place at the end of the class period). You also inform her at this time that if she does not make substantial progress, defining explicitly what that means, she will be removed from the class. This is not a threat. It is a promise of consequences delivered using "You have a choice" and following all the guidelines discussed in Chapter 8. For example, the message should be delivered assertively and respectfully in the proper format, "Ashley, you have a choice. You raise your hand, stay in your seat, and not make fun of Lee, or you will be removed from the class. You decide."

At this point, you enter the details of this meeting into the anecdotal record and ask Ashley to read and then sign the record. Most students now get the message that this is an extremely serious situation and that they are going to be strictly held accountable for their disruptive behavior. Without much fanfare, they sign it and you excuse them from the conference with a thank you and a sincere message that you feel that their behavior will become more appropriate.

However, some students become very resistant and defiant at this point and resort to the display of distorted power. They may say things like, "This is really stupid. I'm not signing anything," or "You gotta be nuts if you think I'm signing this," or "You can do whatever you want, but forget it. I'm not signing this now and certainly not everyday." If this occurs, remember your Post-It, "The only behavior you can control is your own." With this in mind, do not start hollering or berating the student. If you do, you turn this technique from a logical consequence of the student's disruptive behavior to a punishment which then focuses the student's attention on you rather than where it belongs, on themselves. Instead, calmly and respectfully, record verbatim what the student said on the anecdotal record, thank them for coming, and communicate the positive expectations which you have for their improved behavior. An example of an anecdotal record at this point in the hierarchy may look similar to the one in Figure 9.6.

Student Name: <u>Ashley</u>

Phone Number: _____

DATE	STUDENT BEHAVIOR and RESPONSE TO INTERVENTION	TEACHER ACTION	STUDENT SIGNATURE
2/19	1. Ashley arrived late to class 2. began to participate in class 3. called out that Lee's answer was stupid 4. Passed notes to Valerie and refused to work with Taylor	1. said nothing to her, will talk with her after class 2. called on her frequently, used her answers to continue lesson 3. made eye contact with her 4. used proximity control 5. spoke with her after class about lateness, she said she will make it on time from now on	
2/20	1. arrived late to class 2. made fun of Lee 3. got up and took Valerie's paper 4. raised hand to answer 5. hit Tyrone on his arm 6. got up to hit Tyrone again	1. said nothing to her, will speak with her after class 2. eye contact 3. proximity control and asked her to return paper 4. called on her 5. used "you have a choice" 6. intercepted her and told her "she chose to move to the back of the room" 7. spoke to her after class about her lateness and her hitting, problem solved and said she would count to ten when she wanted to hit 8. shared the anecdotal record	
2/21	1. came to class on time 2. got up to hit Tyrone 3. Tyrone said that her answer wasn't right and she got up and hit him.	1. greeted her with a smile 2. I looked at her and said "ten," she sat down 3. told her that she has again decided to move to the back of the room, she moved but was quite verbal about it	

DATE	STUDENT BEHAVIOR and RESPONSE TO INTERVENTION	TEACHER ACTION	STUDENT SIGNATURE
		4. set up a conference with Ashley during lunch 5. discussed self-monitoring where she would make ten checks when she wanted to hit someone 6. shared the anecdotal record	
2/22	1. came to class on time 2. got out of her seat numerous times and took other students' papers 3. got out of her seat and took Vance's papers. When he complained she threw them at him and said she would get him after school because she can't hit anyone in school	1. greeted her with a smile 2. saw her during class make ten marks on her sheet, smiled at her and shook my head yes 3. proximity control, followed by a demand, she returned to her seat, used "You have a choice" when it happened again 4. told her she chose to move to the back of the room and to meet with me after school 5. at our conference explained the idea of a contract. She listened and said it was stupid and she wasn't promising anything. 6. I shared the anecdotal record with her. She said that " the contract is stupid and I'm not going to do it." 7. explained that I was going to continue the record and that she was to read it and sign it each day before she left my class. She said, "No way. I'm never signing this." and she refused to sign it 8. told her that I expected more appropriate behavior and thanked her for coming.	

Figure 9.6 *Sample Anecdotal Record*

The effectiveness of this technique depends upon the consistent recording of daily behavior and the student's signature. If at any time the student refuses to sign the record, like Ashley, just record it. In this manner you are communicating that the student is solely responsible for her behavior and you, the teacher, are merely an impartial recorder of observed behavior. The signature is not the important issue here. What is important is the student's improved behavior, which usually occurs with time, especially if you are conscientious in recording not only the disruptive behavior but also the appropriate behavior of the student. If the behavior is improving and the student refuses to sign it, that's fine; it's probably the student's last attempts at exerting distorted power.

Many teachers when presented with this technique anticipate that it will consume too much time; however this is not the case. The daily recording is done during the last few minutes of class, which is often the time that students are getting ready to leave, copying their homework, or completing the class work. However, there is a concept called conservation of time. In other words, you have a choice. You can spend the time to maintain the anecdotal record or spend the time continually attempting to manage a chronically disruptive student. You decide.

There are no hard and fast rules concerning when to stop using the anecdotal record. When the student has displayed behaviors within the acceptable limits over a number of days, it is appropriate to discuss with the student whether the record keeping continues to be necessary or should be discontinued and encourage the student to continue to behave appropriately. If the behavior is intermittently appropriate and then disruptive, or there is a slight reduction in the degree of disruptiveness, it may be worthwhile to request another private conference with the student and discuss whether the record should be continued a little longer. However, if there is no notable change in the student's behavior within a few days, the record is discontinued and the student is conditionally removed from the class.

Although teachers voice valid concerns about how students may react to this very confrontational technique and about the previously mentioned time issue, keeping anecdotal records is a technique that has been shown to be quite effective in managing chronically disruptive students (Levin et al., 1985, Levin and Nolan, 1996).

Conditional Removal From Class

No student can be allowed to continue to disrupt the learning process for other students indefinitely. Let's take a look at Ashley's situation. The teacher, at this point, attempted to prevent disruptive behavior by increasing Ashley's success/failure ratio, enhancing her intrinsic motivation, and facilitating her development of pro-social self-esteem. In addition, she intervened nonverbally by planned ignoring, signal interference, and proximity interference and verbally by inferential statements and demands. In addition, the teacher delivered logical consequences on numerous occasions and worked individually with Ashley on self-monitoring, problem solving, and anecdotal records. Each intervention was delivered with respect and with the expectation of a positive outcome. Regrettably, at this time Ashley can no longer be a member of the class until she makes a written commitment to behave appropriately in the classroom.

In a private conference with Ashley the teacher explains, "Ashley you have continually disregarded the rights of your fellow classmates to learn by making fun of them, taking their papers, and hitting them. Therefore, at this time you are no longer a member of the class. You are welcome back to our classroom as soon as you provide me with a written promise that you will behave appropriately. Tomorrow, please report to Mr. Black's room." Because this technique removes the student from her assigned classroom, it requires both the approval and support of the administration and the cooperation of another teacher.

Whenever possible, the student should be placed in a classroom with older students. It is generally the case that placing a disruptive student with older students has a tendency to diminish disruptive behavior. In addition, students tend to be less disruptive when they are in unfamiliar surroundings, so even if the student is in the highest grade, just putting her in a different class that is not learning the same material will have a tendency to reduce her disruptive behavior. While the teacher who accepts Ashley into her class may not be delighted to have her, we encourage you to form partnerships with like minded teachers so that they too have an outlet for very disruptive students when necessary. Other locations to which the student may be sent are the principal's, guidance counselor's, or departmental office. We do not recommend sending the student to rooms that have been specially set aside for the sole purpose of housing students who are placed on in-school suspension or for other disciplinary purposes. These rooms tend to exhibit a climate of punishment, exactly what we are trying to avoid.

It is made clear to Ashley that she is still responsible for all work and assignments even though she is not in the room. Therefore, the teacher has the responsibility to provide Ashley with the class assignments each day she is out of the class. Even at this point, the teacher respects Ashley's right to fail and to make the poor choice of remaining oppositional, even if the teacher is now extremely displeased with Ashley's choices.

If Ashley writes a promise of more appropriate behavior, she rejoins the class and starts anew. You want Ashley to know that her past is not being held against her. Any disruptive behaviors that may occur are dealt with from the beginning of the management hierarchy with non-verbal interventions, even though this time the teacher may move more rapidly through the interventions. This helps to mitigate the failure experience of being removed from the class by reaffirming your positive regard and renewed expectation in her ability to use pro-social competence and power to control her behavior in appropriate ways.

There is always the chance that Ashley will not make the written commitment for positive behavior change or she may become disruptive in her new classroom. If a commitment is not forthcoming within three days or she becomes disruptive in the other classroom, the teacher immediately arranges for a parent-teacher conference.

Parent/Teacher Conferences

When it is apparent to the teacher that her interventions have not resulted in appreciable positive change in the student's behavior, parents must be contacted. It may seem a contradiction to conventional wisdom that we include parent/teacher conferences at this point, near the end of the intervention hierarchy. Many educators would argue that parents should be contacted at the very first signs of a discipline problem; however this violates the overall approach of this book. Think for a moment how the average parent of a difficult student behaves when confronted with the fact that their child is disrupting your class. It is our experience that the parent reacts with a sense of embarrassment and anger. It is the rare parent who successfully manages these feelings and avoids the use of very coercive behavior at home in an attempt to force the student into compliance. This is exactly what you have been trying to avoid, because rewards and punishments focus the student's attention away from her behavior and toward her parent's behavior. Next, think how Ashley feels when you contact her parents. She is likely to also feel betrayed, embarrassed, and angry. Once again, her focus is on your behavior rather than on where it should be, her behavior.

Many parents of chronically disruptive students have negative attitudes toward their child's teachers and school in general. This is unfortunate because parental support of school has a major impact on students' positive attitudes toward school (Jones, 1980). Negative parent attitudes result in part, because chronic behavior problems rarely occur overnight. Most likely throughout the student's school years, her parents have had many previous teacher contacts concerning their child's behavior. In addition, it is unfortunate that many chronically disruptive students have parents who also may have had behavior problems when they were in school. Therefore, contacting parents about their child's behavior is often the least desirable and most difficult aspect of a teacher's job. It is the professional, highly-skilled teacher who remains positive and respectful when parents tell teachers, "You should be able to control her; that's why you're getting paid 45,000 dollars a year," or "I've tried everything I know to get Ashley to behave. I give up." Remember, it is your job not only to inform the parents about the problems you are having with Ashley's behavior, but also to encourage the parents to become cooperative partners with you and other school staff members to help Ashley learn and choose more appropriate behavior. As was discussed in Chapters 1 and 3, the teacher increases the probability of this occurring if she safeguards herself from personalizing the parent's behavior, just like she has worked hard on not personalizing the student's behavior. The message to the parents from the teacher is, "How can we work together to help Ashley?" and not, "We have done all we can. Now it's up to you."

In addition, parents are much more supportive of the teacher's efforts if previous to this contact the teacher routinely involved parents in more positive aspects of the school and their child's education. This is why schoolwide programs such as back-to-school night, volunteer programs, parenting workshops, parent-teacher organizations, and parent advisory boards are so very important. Teachers may supplement these programs with invitations to visit or volunteer in the classroom, sending "good news" notes home, phoning parents to inform them of their children's progress, and generally making themselves available to parents when any concerns arise.

Although not specifically covered as a separate intervention, when the teacher has approached this point in the hierarchy, she usually has consulted with the school counselor and/or a school administrator; it is also likely that the student has seen the counselor and/or the principal or vice-principal. These staff members may play a vital role in managing the student's behavior. For example, the counselor, being an outside observer, can visit the classroom and provide objective feedback to the teacher on new approaches for working with the student, while at the same time working with the student to develop more acceptable behavior. Additionally, the counselor may help to improve the strained teacher-student relationship that most likely exists at this time. Administrators must also be consulted if there is a possibility that the student may be placed permanently in another classroom, assigned to specialized educational settings in or outside the school, or referred to other professionals such as a school or private psychologist.

Once the conference is scheduled, it is important that the teacher and any other school staff member who will be present decide to make the meeting, as much as possible, a positive experience for the parents. The decision of who will attend the conference needs to be made. The answer depends on the particular problem and the expertise needed to answer parents' questions. Keep in mind that you want an atmosphere that is the least intimidating to the parents; therefore we suggest as few people as possible. Students are always present unless the discussion involves serious concerns about health, home, or legal problems. The parents should be notified who will attend the conference prior to the meeting.

Professional behavior must be practiced by all school staff at all times. Parents' views should be encouraged and respected, and at no time should the student or parents be attacked, blamed, or in any other manner be put on the defensive. Only when the parents feel less threatened and blamed, can they fully participate in the sought after cooperative school/ parent team approach that is needed to help their child. The conference should have a serious tone but always with the focus being on positive outcomes for the student.

One very important aspect of professional behavior is the use of data in decision making. This is why the anecdotal record the teacher has been keeping on Ashley is so important. The record provides a longitudinal documentation of Ashley's behaviors and the interventions the teacher has employed. These data 1) reduce the likelihood of the conference eroding into a debate, 2) illustrate the seriousness of the problem, and 3) defuse any attempts by the parents to suggest the teacher or the school has not taken proper and necessary actions (Levin and Nolan, 1996).

During the conference, the teacher may be called upon to explain and defend her decision not to contact the parents earlier. It is at this time that the teacher needs to educate the parents about her philosophy. This is why early in the book it was stressed that if you understand the *whys,* you can design the *hows.* It is now time to explain to the parents the *whys.* It is important for the parents to understand who they can and can not control. It must be stressed that they do not have total control over their child and they are not bad parents because their child is disruptive in school. Our experience is that parents greet this news with a welcome sense of relief. This new understanding is not meant to communicate to the parents that they have no responsibility with respect to Ashley's behavior because in fact they do. However, the responsibility is not *for* Ashley, but it is *to* Ashley. Their responsibility to Ashley is in deciding how they choose to cooperate and interact with the teacher and school to encourage Ashley towards more appropriate behavior.

The outcome of the meeting needs to be a decision as to what are the next appropriate interventions. With some students, the decision is for the teacher and/or the school to try more interventions with little or no additional parental involvement. This outcome usually results because the meeting uncovers information about the student that enables the teacher and/or the school to design and implement strategies not previously considered. Unfortunately, it may also be the outcome when parents show a real disinterest in their child or any additional involvement. With other students, the teacher's decision may be to request additional parental involvement such as integrative routines where the intervention strategies used in school are also the same strategies used at home. Others strategies may be daily progress reports or even participation by the parents in effective parenting classes. It may also be decided that consultation or referrals to other professionals within or outside the school is necessary.

At Ashley's parent/teacher conference, she, her parents, and her teacher decided on the teacher sending home daily progress reports of her behavior. In addition, her parents and the professional school staff decided to explore consultation with other outside professionals.

Referral to Outside Professionals

The last intervention in the hierarchy is referral to outside professionals. It is last because it is the only intervention that is discussed which the teacher does not implement in the classroom, and the intervention is not a direct interaction between the teacher and the student.

If this point in the hierarchy is reached, the teacher may likely perceive herself as having failed. Rationally this is not a failure. After all, the teacher has no control over Ashley's ongoing choice to be disruptive. Most likely the causes of Ashley's continued disruptive behavior have nothing to do with what the teacher has or has not done. The teacher controlled her behavior using best professional practice. Like a competent medical doctor who refers her patients to specialists, it is the competent educator who recognizes when a student's behavior is outside the teacher's expertise and who initiates the referral process.

Different school districts have different referral processes. Sometimes the referral is initiated by the teacher, other times by the school counselor or school psychologist. Some schools have instructional support teams or child study teams who make the referral.

In many cases the first referrals are made within the school district to the district's learning specialist or psychologist. Your input, and particularly Ashley's anecdotal record, is valuable data for these individuals as they attempt to understand Ashley's problem and to work with her to help her make appropriate changes in her behavior.

In cases where it is deemed necessary, the student may be referred to specialists other than district personnel. We encourage schools and teachers to familiarize themselves with the philosophies and approaches of the counseling and psychological services in the community so that a proper referral can be made. For example, referring a student to a behavioral psychologist who designs systems of classroom rewards and punishment will be contradictory to your philosophy and techniques, if you subscribe to the approach detailed in this book. In addition, referrals should be made to those individuals who are active in schools and knowledgeable about how classrooms operate, particularly in regard to classroom management. A psychologist or counselor who does not have frequent contact with schools and teachers is unlikely to be able to successfully impact classroom behavior of students.

To the degree that you remain involved with Ashley and in contact with her parents and with the outside professionals with whom she is working, Ashley is more likely to learn how to control her behavior within acceptable limits and experience a success/failure ratio > 1, develop intrinsic motivation, and display pro-social self-esteem.

SYMPTOMS OF SERIOUS PROBLEMS THAT NEED IMMEDIATE REFERRAL

Some students may display symptoms that are indicative of serious physical or emotional problems, or associated with substance abuse or home abuse. These symptoms may or may not be accompanied by disruptive behavior. All of these fall outside the expertise and responsibility of the teacher. However, it is incumbent upon, and in some states the law requires, teachers to report these symptoms to appropriate school officials, who are knowledgeable regarding the next steps.

Some of the symptoms are noticeable changes in 1) physical appearance, 2) activity level, 3) personality, 4) achievement status, 5) health, 6) socialization, 7) physical abilities, and 8) any appearances of unusual burns, bruises, or abrasions.

SUMMARY

This chapter presents the last level of the intervention hierarchy. It poses a most difficult challenge: how can one intervene with chronically disruptive students, while at the same time protecting or facilitating their success/failure ratio and encouraging whatever degree of intrinsic motivation and pro-social self-esteem they may have? Since the temptation at this point may be to assign negative labels to these students, teachers are reminded of the negative effects of labeling.

Before using any of the interventions covered in this chapter, two teacher preparatory procedures were detailed. The first intervention, one that is invaluable for effectively intervening with chronically disruptive students, is the anecdotal record. This daily record documents both student and teacher behavior. The second is the Teacher Individual Management Action Plan, a self-analysis of the history of teacher intervention with the disruptive student.

There are eight interventions in this last level of the hierarchy. As with the entire hierarchy, and within each of the previous levels, these interventions are ordered from least confrontational to most confrontational. The movement through this level and the determination of the number of techniques to employ are functions of both the degree of disruptiveness of the student's behavior and of the amount of sincere student effort toward displaying appropriate behavior.

The eight interventions are 1) teacher/student conference, 2) student self-monitoring, 3) student problem solving, 4) contracting for change, 5) anecdotal record keeping with student participation, 6) conditional removal from class, 7) parent/teacher conference, and 8) referral to outside professionals. By continuing to make professional decisions, by communicating your belief that the student has the ability to behave appropriately, by focusing on the student's behavior and not the student's character, and by respecting the student's right to choose how she will behave, the teacher increases the probability that these techniques will be effective.

Lastly, some students exhibit symptoms of serious physical or psychological problems which may or may not be accompanied by disruptive behavior. Teachers need to recognize these symptoms and report these potentially serious problems to the appropriate school official.

Concept Map

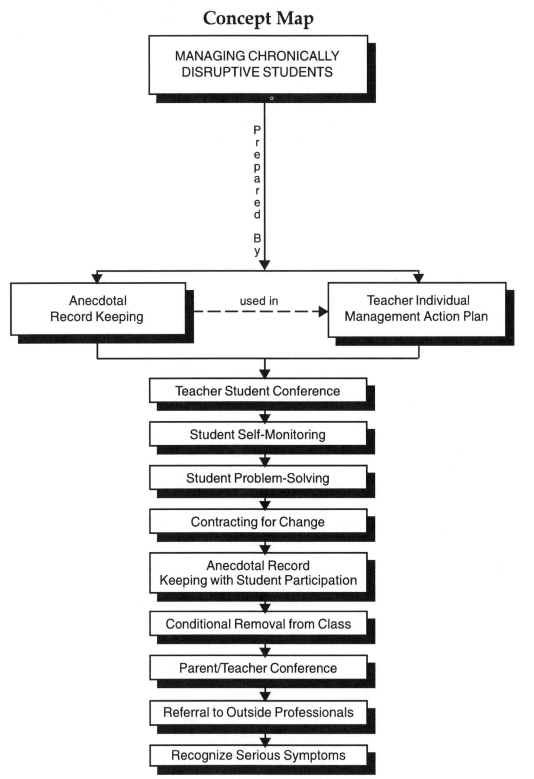

MANAGING CHRONICALLY DISRUPTIVE STUDENTS

Prepared By

Anecdotal Record Keeping — used in → Teacher Individual Management Action Plan

Teacher Student Conference

Student Self-Monitoring

Student Problem-Solving

Contracting for Change

Anecdotal Record Keeping with Student Participation

Conditional Removal from Class

Parent/Teacher Conference

Referral to Outside Professionals

Recognize Serious Symptoms

REFERENCES

Brendtro, L. K., Brokenleg, M., and Van Bockern, S. (1990). *Reclaiming Youth at Risk: Our Hope for the Future.* Bloomington, IN: National Educational Service.

Jones, V. F. (1980). *Adolescents with Behavior Problems.* Boston: Allyn and Bacon.

Levin, J. and Nolan, J. F. (1996). *Principles of Classroom Management: A Professional Decision Making Model,* second edition, Boston: Allyn and Bacon.

Levin, J., Nolan, J. F., and Hoffman, N. (1985). A strategy for the classroom resolution of chronic discipline problems. *National Association of Secondary School Principals Bulletin, 69,* 479, 11-18.

FREQUENTLY ASKED QUESTIONS

1. What should you do if you ask a chronically disruptive student to remain after class to discuss her behavior and the first words out of her mouth are "You know, I'm acting up in class just to make your life miserable and nothing you can do will stop me."

2. What can you do when working with a chronically disruptive student in a school where the administration does not want to be bothered by discipline problems?

3. What should be done if parents refuse to come in for a conference?

4. "I once had a situation where at the completion of a parent/teacher conference the father got up to leave, slapped the student across the face, and said, 'You won't have any future problems with her!' What should I have done?"

5. What do I do when a student's private therapist recommends techniques to influence the student's behavior with which I disagree?

6. What do I do if none of these techniques work?

Epilogue

Presently there are more students with severe and chronic discipline problems in our schools than ever before. This fact coupled with the other demands on teachers, such as keeping up with the knowledge explosion, inclusion, and cutbacks in funding, create tremendous pressure and stress on the classroom teacher. Being an excellent teacher is harder than it has ever been.

We have attempted in this book to provide a philosophy that can help teachers to ameliorate the stress of their job. Two major tenets of this philosophy are: the only one you can control is yourself, and you do not have responsibility for students—you have responsibility to students. We have throughout suggested that these tenets be put in practice by controlling your behavior to be respectful of all students and by using management and instructional techniques that continually encourage students to choose appropriate rather than disruptive behavior. This is best accomplished not by rewards and punishments, but by setting high expectations for all students, using encouragement and effective instruction to prevent disruptive behavior, and by using pre-planned, management interventions which respect student power and choice when disruptive behavior occurs

A wise teacher explained it to the authors this way, "In today's schools a teacher cannot base her feelings of competency on how students achieve or behave. Instead she must base her feelings on what she does each day to encourage achievement and appropriate behavior. Everyday I ask myself, 'Am I proud of the way I taught today?' and 'Would I want my own child to be in a classroom taught by a teacher like me?' If I answer "yes" to both questions, I know I've done a good job. If I answer "no" to either question, well I know tomorrow is a new day, and I can try again.'

Definitions of Success/Failure Ratio, Motivitation, and Self-Esteem

SUCCESS/FAILURE RATIO

1. The success/failure ratio is a measure of an individual's self-worth as determined by the ratio of their successful experiences to their failure experiences.
   a. S/F > 1 denotes many more successful experiences than failure experiences.
   b. S/F < 1 denotes many more failure experiences than successful experiences.

MOTIVATION

1. Motivation is a measure of an individual's will to initiate and to put forth effort in activities from which some gain is sought.
2. Motivation is defined as the Expectation of Success multiplied by Value.
3. M = E x V
   a. Expectation of Success is the belief an individual has that she can attain a desired goal.
   b. Value is the importance of the goal to the individual.
4. Motivation can be intrinsic or extrinsic.
   a. Intrinsic Motivation is defined as an Internal Locus of Control multiplied by an Internal Value Structure
   b. Intrinsic Motivation = Internal Locus of Control x Internal Value Structure
      1) An individual has an Internal Locus of Control when the individual's expectation of success is dependent upon factors within the individual's control (i.e. effort, ability).
      2) An Internal Value Structure exists when the outcomes valued by the individual are independent of the participation of others (i.e.competence, interest).
   c. Extrinsic Motivation is defined as an Extrinsic Locus of Control multiplied by an Extrinsic Value Structure
   d. Extrinsic Motivation = External Locus of Control x External Value Structure
      1) An individual has an External Locus of Control when the individual's expectation of success is dependent upon factors outside the individual's control (i.e. luck, type of teacher).
      2) An External Value Structure exists when the outcomes valued by the individual are dependent on the participation of others (i.e. rewards, show superiority).

SELF-ESTEEM

1. Self-Esteem is defined as the sum of Significance, Competence, Virtue, and Power.
2. $SE = S + C + V + P$
   a. Significance is an individual's belief that she is respected, liked, and trusted by people who are important to her.
   b. Competence is an individual's sense of mastery in tasks that she values.
   c. Virtue is an individual's perceived feeling of worthiness as a result of her ability and willingness to help others.
   d. Power is an individual's perception that she exerts control over important aspects of her environment.
3. Self-Esteem can be Pro-Social or Distorted
   a. Pro-Social Self-Esteem is self-esteem obtained through socially acceptable means.

   1) $SE_{ps} = S_{ps} + C_{ps} + V_{ps} + P_{ps}$

   b. Distorted Self-Esteem is self-esteem obtained through antisocial means.

   1) $SE_d = S_d + C_d + V_d + P_d$

Heirarchy of
Management Interventions

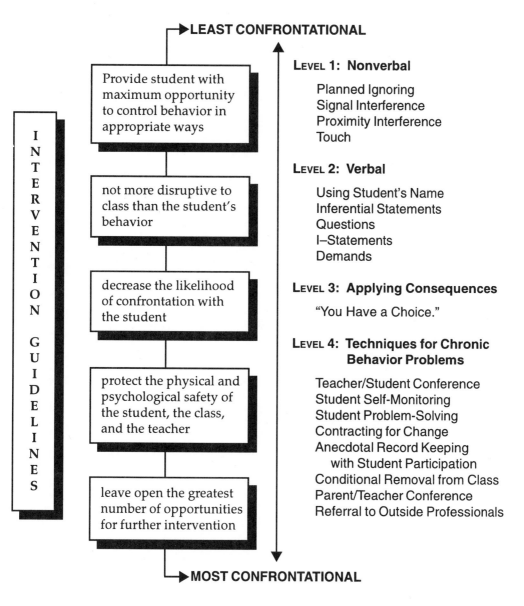

LEAST CONFRONTATIONAL

Provide student with maximum opportunity to control behavior in appropriate ways

not more disruptive to class than the student's behavior

decrease the likelihood of confrontation with the student

protect the physical and psychological safety of the student, the class, and the teacher

leave open the greatest number of opportunities for further intervention

INTERVENTION GUIDELINES

LEVEL 1: Nonverbal

Planned Ignoring
Signal Interference
Proximity Interference
Touch

LEVEL 2: Verbal

Using Student's Name
Inferential Statements
Questions
I–Statements
Demands

LEVEL 3: Applying Consequences

"You Have a Choice."

LEVEL 4: Techniques for Chronic Behavior Problems

Teacher/Student Conference
Student Self-Monitoring
Student Problem-Solving
Contracting for Change
Anecdotal Record Keeping
    with Student Participation
Conditional Removal from Class
Parent/Teacher Conference
Referral to Outside Professionals

MOST CONFRONTATIONAL

Index of Persons

Index

Workshop/Seminar Information

James Levin and John Shanken–Kaye are available to provide customized workshops and professional inservice instruction to your school district, school, professional, parent, or advocacy group or company. These dynamic speakers make the information presented in the Self-Control Classroom immediate and compelling to any group interested in the behavioral problems many children experience. Inservice can also be offered for graduate or continuing professional education credit through Penn State University Continuing and Distance Education.

Topics include:

→ Classroom Management and Effective Instruction
→ Classroom Management of Chronically Disruptive Students
→ School-Wide Discipline
→ Self-Esteem and Motivation
→ Proud Parents/Proud Kids: a highly effective parenting program based on the theories presented in the The Self-Control Classroom.

Please contact Levin/Shanken–Kaye Associates to receive information on your topic(s) of interest by completing the postcard, calling 1-215-938-1765, or e-mailing at shank@voicenet.com